SENT OR SOLD

THE DREAMER'S DILEMMA

RONALD E. CHIPP

Phullon Publishing LLC

Published by:

Phullon Publishing LLC
P.O. Box 5329
Saginaw, Michigan 48603

Cover Art: Jill Case

www.phullon.com

978-1-939471-03-1

Unless otherwise indicated, all scripture quotations are
from the King James Version of the Bible.

DEDICATION

I affectionately dedicate this book to my loving wife, Phyllis, who has been a faithful source of inspiration and encouragement.

I also dedicate this book to my children, Aaron (Tamar) and Autumn (Darrell) who bring me much delight.

Finally, I dedicate this book to Faith Harvest Church and its leadership. Your support of me, my family, and ministry, has strengthened my life.

Foreword

Sent or Sold: The Dreamer's Dilemma should be in every dreamer's arsenal. It is a strong weapon against the enemies of doubt, despair, and discouragement, during the inevitable twists and turns of your journey, to fulfillment of your God-given dreams and visions. With the love and persistence of a supportive father, Bishop Ronald Chipp encourages the reader to never give up, but instead, to look up. That is, to see your circumstances from God's perspective. Through an obvious love and knowledge of the Scriptures, coupled with the keen insight into the heart and purposes of God, Bishop Chipp does what he does best, he teaches with wisdom and revelation. He has a rare ability to impart not just knowledge, but also understanding. His love for God and God's word are evident throughout this book. What is also evident is his sincere desire that every dreamer gain a heart of wisdom in the triumphant pursuit of divine destiny.

As a husband, father, pastor, and bishop, Ronald Chipp knows that attitude is key to success. He has learned by experience, and taught out of love, that the right attitude is key to achieving goals. I recall a time when my husband and I were hiking in the Sierra Nevada Mountains with a group of seven other people. The climb early on became far more difficult than I anticipated. Even though this had been a dream of mine since high school (Ron and I were celebrating our 29th wedding anniversary on this journey into the mountains), I was ready to quit and return home in defeat. As I struggled up a steep incline with a heavy pack on my back, gasping for breath, and struggling as much or more mentally, than I was physically, I stopped and broke down in tears. It was too much for me. I was done. I could not go another step. For me, at that moment, the climb was over, and my dream was crushed. It was then, that I heard a soft but determined voice behind me. "You can do this Phyl. Stop and catch your breath. You are not holding up the rest of us, we all need a breather. You are going to make it, and every day you are going to get stronger." I heard my husband's voice as the voice of God at that moment. He didn't remove the load from my back (that wasn't the answer); he removed the load from my mind. Like a strong but gentle coach, he helped me quickly adjust my attitude. This attitude adjustment made all the difference. Not only did I go on to finish the climb, but I did grow stronger each day. That time in the mountains ranks as one of the most joyous times in my life, and what I learned about mental toughness (a right attitude), has led me on many adventures around the world since then.

Reading this book will help you no matter where you are on your "climb" to fulfill your dreams and visions. This book will be that confident, and determined voice behind you, encouraging you to keep moving, letting you know that you are going to make it, that you are not alone. You will keep the fire of your dreams alive and burning brightly. Sent or Sold: The Dreamer's Dilemma will be that voice, speaking to your heart, like the voice of God.

Phyllis Chipp

Table of Contents

Chapter 1

THE DREAMER'S DILEMMA

It's exciting to see our dreams and visions begin to come to pass. I believe every person, has a God-given dream inside of them. They may not recognize it, or it may lie dormant, but I believe it is there in all of us. Big dreams and visions often come with big problems, challenges, and obstacles. Every conscious dreamer and visionary soon learns that the path to destiny is cluttered with dilemmas and dream threatening obstacles. Many people abort their dreams and forfeit their destiny because they have not resolved what I call "The Dreamers Dilemma!"

The Dreamer's Dilemma is well seen in the life of the patriarch Joseph. A dilemma can be defined as: A predicament that seemingly defies a satisfactory solution. The usage of the word dilemma is sometimes loosely used of any problem. It denotes a problem which poses two alternatives, each of which must be carefully weighed. The "Dreamers Dilemma" involves the problem of discerning, and deciding, which attitude he or she will have in life! We sometimes say, "That person has an attitude!" More often than not, we mean they have an unpleasant or bad attitude. The truth is, we all have an attitude! The challenge is recognizing, and choosing which attitude we will have in life. Attitude is a destiny decider! It can be a destiny destroyer, or a circumstance conqueror!

This book gives a bold and fresh new look at the life of Joseph, the biblical patriarch, and the power of attitude. The power of a "sent" attitude will be unveiled, and bring you face-to-face with your own attitude in life. Like Joseph, dreamers and visionaries face many dilemmas and obstacles in pursuit of destiny.

As we look at the life of Joseph, I believe the power of a "sent" attitude, will be released, strengthened, and encouraged in your life. I also believe, you will find resolution to your own dilemmas in life, and strengthen your heart, and attitude, to overcome all the dream threatening obstacles you are facing.

Like Joseph, we must decide what our attitude in life is going to be! No matter how great or inspiring our dreams and visions may be, we will always face circumstances, and situations, that seem to contradict the reality of the belief we hold in our hearts concerning our future. Joseph received a dream from God that prophesied his exaltation, and success in life as a leader. However, when you look at the life of Joseph, especially in the beginning, it seemed as if his life was headed in the opposite direction! Joseph undoubtedly had to make a decision concerning what his attitude in life would be.

One of the many challenges that Joseph faced in his life was that he was sold into slavery. God knew a famine would come upon the land, so He sent Joseph to Egypt, to raise him up as a leader, with the wisdom to lead Egypt, and other nations during that difficult time. The Bible, which is the word of God, also tells us that Joseph was sold into slavery.

He _SENT_ [my emphasis] a man before them, even Joseph, who was _SOLD_ [my emphasis] for a servant; Whose feet they hurt with fetters: he was laid in iron:

Psalm 105:17-18

Notice the scripture above says Joseph was both, "sent" and "sold." It presents what seems to be a dilemma in his life. Joseph was sent to Egypt by God, even though Joseph's circumstances said he was sold! At some point in time Joseph had to decide what his attitude in life would be. The "Dreamer's Dilemma is: "Am I sent or sold; am I sent by

God or sold under my circumstances?" The "Dreamer's Dilemma" begs the question, "Do I have a sent or sold attitude?" Joseph had to choose between a "sent" or "sold" attitude!

As you pursue your God-given dreams and visions, you must decide what your attitude in life will be. When your circumstances or situation is different, or even contrary to what God or His word says, what will you believe, and what will your attitude be? Some people allow their circumstances to determine their attitude, instead of allowing a "sent" attitude to dominate their circumstances. Don't allow your circumstances to dictate your attitude!

A Sold Attitude

A "sold" attitude says, "I am in bondage to my circumstances!" The word attitude can be defined as the disposition and feeling with regard to a person or thing; inclination or propensity, especially of the mind. A "sold" attitude will rob you of your dreams, visions, and destiny because you are not able to see beyond your personal problems or obstacles. A "sold" attitude says, "I have no control, or very little control over my life, and circumstances."

Chapter 1

The root of a "sold" attitude or mentality, is a lack of trust, and commitment to the will and promise of God, in the face of difficulty and hardship.

People with this frame of mind identify more with their limitations and problems, than with their potential, possibilities, and God-given promises. A person with this kind of attitude tends to surrender his or her life to situations and circumstances, when they should surrender to the will of God. The root of a "sold" attitude or mentality, is a lack of trust, and commitment to the will and promise of God, in the face of difficulty and hardship. A "sold" attitude will prophesy and promote defeat in your life!

People with a "sold" attitude tend to think the presence of hardship, difficulty, or obstacles, are always indicators of being out of the will of God. Therefore, they relinquish their dreams and visions to their circumstances. Thank God, we don't have to settle for a "sold" attitude! We can grab hold to a "sent" attitude, and see ourselves as overcomers, and more than conquerors in Christ; right in the midst of difficult circumstances.

A "sent" attitude says, "The hardship and difficulty of my circumstances does not define my dreams, visions, and destiny!"

A Sent Attitude

A "sent" attitude says, "The hardship and difficulty of my circumstances does not define my dreams, visions, and destiny!" It is an attitude, or frame of mind, that focuses on God and His power in our lives; not on the limitations of our circumstances. A "sent" attitude is born out of knowing and pursuing the purposes of God for our lives. People with a "sent" attitude have a genuine relationship with the Supreme Sender in life - God! They believe God has sent them forth to represent Him in life, as light, and the salt of the earth; that they are sent to do good works, even in bad times. People with a "sent" attitude are determined to look beyond the natural (and its limitations) to the supernatural power of God, and the possibilities this affords them.

Your attitude in life acts as a filter in what and how you see things. A good attitude will allow you to see things properly, with integrity and undistorted. A bad attitude will cause a distortion in how you hear, see, and experience things in life. A "sent" attitude will not allow circumstances to distort, and discourage your God-given dreams and visions. It is a disposition in the midst of difficulty, and hardship, that empowers us to maintain integrity and confidence.

> **People with a "sent" attitude are able to see the hand of God at work in their lives, even if they find themselves in a pit or prison.**

People with a "sent" attitude are able to see the hand of God at work in their lives, even if they find themselves in a pit or prison. A "sent" attitude says, "God is with me; He will deliver me; God gives me favor, and He will give me the wisdom necessary to fulfill my dreams, visions, and destiny.

Our God-given destiny is not just about what we accomplish, but also about whom we become!

The Pursuit of Destiny

Dreams and visions are about our destiny. Our God-given destiny is not just about what we accomplish, but also about whom we become!

For whom he did foreknow, he also did predestinate to be conformed to the image of his Son, that he might be the first-born among many brethren.

Romans 8:29

God is just as concerned about our person, as he is about our productivity. It is important to realize that destiny includes being conformed to the image of Jesus Christ. In other words, character development is a vital part of destiny. God-given dreams and visions are born of the Spirit of God and the word of God. They line-up with the word of God! There is a time element to the fulfillment of our dreams and visions.

Chapter 1

Until the time that his word came: the word of the LORD tried him.

Psalm 105:19

While we pursue our dreams and visions, the word of the LORD will try (purify, refine and prove) us. In other words, God will use your challenges, difficulties, and obstacles to forge godly character, and spiritual growth in your life. Sometimes in our focus to bring the dream to pass, and accomplish our visions, we become acutely aware of another aspect of the "dreamer's dilemma!" This is when we become more concerned about "doing" something, then we are about "becoming," the person God wants us to be. Again, God-given destiny is not just about what we accomplish, but also about whom we become!

Only your character can keep you, where your gifts and talents will take you!

Only your character can keep you, where your gifts and talents will take you! Our dreams, visions, gifts, and talents will bring us to an exalted place in life. We need to have the character to handle that place of honor and responsibility.

SENT OR SOLD: THE DREAMER'S DILEMMA

Please understand this; intelligence, gifts, and talents, does not necessarily equate to good character! How many times have we witnessed the rise of people to prominence in sports, acting, business, even ministry, and other areas of life, only to discover their character did not measure up to their stardom (gifts and talents)!

Sometimes for a season, when our focus is on numbers (a bigger ministry or business), God's focus, may be on our attitude, or character growth. It may look like things are just not happening for you, because you are not experiencing the numerical, or financial growth you desire. In reality, you are moving closer to your destiny, because of your attitude and character development, in the face of opposition.

> **It seems like things are only getting worse, when in actuality, we are only getting better as we co-operate with the process of God.**

Sometimes, because we are so focused on the growth of our wealth, business, and ministry, we can't recognize the character growth God is developing in our lives. It seems like things are only getting worse, when in actuality, we are only getting better as we co-operate with the process of God.

Chapter 2

JOSEPH'S STORY

Joseph's father was Jacob (Israel). Jacob favored Joseph above his other children. He even made Joseph a special "coat of many colors." In fact, the Bible says in Genesis, chapter 37, that Jacob loved Joseph more than all his children. Now, my purpose is not to focus on parenting skills, but I think it is important to note that we should love all our children the same! God does! I understand that each of our children is different, and therefore we sometimes have to motivate them differently, because of their various personalities, gifts, and talents. However, as parents we should love all our children the same.

I have seen on more than one occasion where a parent or parents, will love or favor one child over the other. Sometimes the parent doesn't even see it, and sometimes they just don't care. This causes problems in family relationships, especially among siblings. This was the case also with Joseph and his brothers. They hated Joseph because of their father's love and favoritism toward him over them. If you are a parent, I caution you and challenge you to examine your relationship, and love for all your children. Thank God, we don't have to be perfect before God will begin to use us! Jacob had some issues as a son, and he definitely had some issues as a father. Today, the Jacob household would qualify as a "dysfunctional family!"

> **I often say, "We serve a perfect God, who uses imperfect people, to do his perfect will!"**

We are all under construction. I often say, "We serve a perfect God, who uses imperfect people, to do his perfect will!" However, we should always strive for perfection.

Let us get back to Joseph's story. Joseph dreamed a dream, and told it to his brothers. The word of God says his brothers hated him the more because of his dreams. Joseph's dreams often included him being exalted, in authority, and his brothers and parents would have to make obeisance to him. For reason of his dreams, his father first rebuked him, but took notice of them, and his brothers hated and envied him.

Even though our dreams and visions will motivate and inspire us, it does not mean others will feel the same way. Sometimes it takes a while for our own family to see, and embrace our God-given dreams and visions. Like Joseph, we must not allow anyone to steal our dreams. Joseph kept dreaming.

One day when Joseph's brothers were out tending to the flocks, Jacob sent Joseph to go check on them, and to see how things were going. When his brothers saw him coming, they said to one another, "Behold, this dreamer cometh." For reason of their hatred and envy for Joseph, they decided to kill him, throw him in a pit, and tell his father that some evil or wild beast killed him. They also said, "We shall see what will become of his dreams." Thank God for Reuben, the older brother who convinced them not to kill him. Therefore, they took his coat of many colors and then threw him into a pit.

As Joseph's brothers sat down to eat they saw a company of Ishmaelite's from Gilead on their way to Egypt with their camels loaded down with merchandise. Then Judah suggested that they sell Joseph to the Ishmaelite's, because there was no profit in killing him. They all consented, and sold Joseph for twenty pieces of silver, and the Ishmaelite's took him to Egypt. Then they took Joseph's coat of many colors, dipped it in goat's blood, and told their father Jacob, they found it! When Jacob saw the coat covered in blood, he assumed Joseph was dead, and mourned Joseph greatly for many days.

It certainly looks like Joseph's life is headed in the opposite direction of his dreams. In fact, Joseph was sold, not once, but twice! When the Ishmaelite's got to Egypt, they sold Joseph again to Potiphar, an officer of Pharaoh's, and captain of the guard. Twice, Joseph was sold into slavery. About this time, many would think that God had abandoned them, and they would probably never get out from under their circumstances. Perhaps, by now they would have begun to have self-esteem problems, or become mean and bitter.

Joseph however, apparently kept a good attitude and did not become bitter. We see in Genesis, chapter 39, that a good attitude, faith in God, and the blessing of God, will cause you to rise above your circumstances. Even as a slave, the Bible says God was with Joseph, and he was a prosperous man. The word of God says Joseph's master, Potiphar, saw that the LORD was with Joseph, and made all that Joseph did to prosper in his hand. Because of this, Joseph found grace with his master Potiphar, who made Joseph overseer over his house. The Bible goes on to say the LORD blessed the Egyptian's (Potiphar's) house for Joseph's sake! I believe the LORD was able to bless Joseph's life, and the works of his hands, because of his "sent" attitude. In fact, Genesis 39:6 tells us that Joseph was a goodly person and well favored.

> **I believe the LORD was able to bless Joseph's life, and the works of his hands, because of his "sent" attitude.**

Things were looking up for Joseph. Perhaps with such favor and prosperity, Joseph began to dream about his freedom being won or bought. Maybe his God-given dream would happen soon. Well, it wasn't long before Potiphar's wife took a liking to Joseph, and wanted to have sex with him. Joseph, being a man of integrity, and of godly character, refused to do so. She refused to take no for an answer, and continued to pursue him day by day. Finally, she ran out of patience, grabbed Joseph by his clothes, and demanded him to lie with her. Joseph broke loose, leaving his garment in her hand, and fled the house.

Joseph told Potiphar's wife that he could not do such wickedness, and sin against God! I dare say, some men would not have been thinking about God, period! With all that Joseph had gone through, one might be tempted to think this would be a good chance to get back at my slave master, and pleasure myself at the same time. Joseph was more interested in pleasing God, then pleasing himself, or Potiphar's wife!

> **Joseph was more interested in pleasing God, then pleasing himself, or Potiphar's wife!**

Potiphar's wife, because of Joseph's rejection, accused him of attempted rape. After Joseph ran out of the house she called the men of the house, told them he tried to rape her, and showed them his garment as proof. Then she laid up the garment by her side until her husband, Potiphar came home, and told him the same story.

Needless to say, but I will say it anyway, Potiphar was hopping mad! Consequently, he put Joseph in prison. Thank God for his grace! Generally, that kind of accusation and wrath can easily get somebody dead, if you know what I mean.

Joseph is again at a place in his life where he must address the "Dreamer's Dilemma:" Am I sent or sold? Did things just get better or worse? Am I getting closer to the fulfillment of my dream, or am I getting farther away from it? Is this holiness and integrity stuff really worth all this suffering? I believe Joseph had a conviction that he was "sent" and not "sold!" The Bible tells us that the LORD was with Joseph in prison, showed him mercy, and gave him favor with the keeper of the prison. Like Potiphar, the keeper of the prison committed all the prisoners to Joseph's hand. The LORD was with him, and whatever he did, God made it to prosper.

**What looked like
a major setback
was a major setup,
by God!**

Sometimes what seems to be the worst position, with God, therein is your best potential. Sometimes when it seems as though you are bound by your biggest obstacle, with God, therein lay your greatest opportunity! For such it was with Joseph. In Genesis, chapter 40, we learn it was in the confines of imprisonment that Joseph's gifts, talents, and wisdom to interpret dreams, were exercised, and brought to Pharaoh's attention. What looked like a major setback was a major setup, by God!

SENT OR SOLD: THE DREAMER'S DILEMMA

Our attitude acts as a filter, greatly affecting what we can see with the eyes of our understanding. With the right attitude, a "sent" attitude, even in the darkness of a dungeon, you can see a "set-up!" This explains why, after Joseph had interpreted a dream for the chief butler, that had fallen out of favor with Pharaoh, (that he would be restored to his position); Joseph told the butler to remember him, and mention him to Pharaoh so he could get out of prison. I believe Joseph's attitude allowed him to see a set-up! Joseph expected God to deliver him from bondage. Joseph expected the manifestation of God's favor in his life.

Envy, the Dreamer's Assassin

A major enemy to our dreams and visions is envy. Joseph's brothers hated him because of their father's favoritism and for his dreams. Joseph's dream revealed his future success and exaltation over his brothers.

Now Israel (Jacob) loved Joseph more than all his children, because he was the son of his old age: and he made him a coat of many colours. And when his brethren saw that their father loved him more than all his brethren, they hated him, and could not speak peaceably unto him. And Joseph dreamed a dream, and he told it his brethren: and they hated him yet the more. And his brethren said to him, Shalt

thou indeed reign over us? Or shall thou indeed have dominion over us? And they hated him yet the more for his dreams, and for his words. And his brethren ENVIED [my emphasis] him; but his Father observed the saying.

Genesis 37:3-5,8,11

Envy is resentment against another's success. It is a first cousin to hate! Envy is always accompanied with some degree of hatred, or ill will, with the desire or effort, to depreciate the person it is directed to. In fact, envy takes pleasure in seeing its target depressed, and at a disadvantage. Envy brings emotional pain to those who have it. It causes uneasiness and discontentment, because of the real, or perceived superior excellence, reputation, or happiness enjoyed by another.

I think it is interesting to note that the Latin word for envy is "invideo." It literary means, to see against, that is, to look at with enmity. People with envy in their heart, get upset at the very sight of a person they think enjoys some advantage that they do not! We see this dynamic in the life of Joseph and his brothers. When Joseph went out to check on his brothers for his father Jacob, they saw him coming.

And when they <u>SAW</u> [my emphasis] him afar off, even before he came near unto them, they <u>CONSPIRED</u> [my emphasis] against him to slay him. And they said one to another, Behold, this dreamer cometh.

Genesis 37:18-19

Joseph's brothers became emotionally upset at the mere sight of him. Joseph was not even near them yet, and they began to hate on him! He didn't even get a chance to speak, or tell them why he was there. Envy is the dreamer's assassin! Joseph's brothers conspired to kill him. They said among themselves, look, that dreamer is coming.

Envy is the dreamer's Assassin!

An assassin is one who kills or attempts to kill, by surprise, or secret assault. Notice Joseph's brothers conspired to kill him (Genesis 37: 18). Secrecy and surprise seem to be essential to the work of assassins. Joseph's brothers wanted to assassinate him because of his dreams. Satan will use people who have envy in their heart, to try and assassinate you, and your God-given dreams. They will attempt to assassinate your character, ministry, or business. Some people will even try to physically kill you.

The enemy (the devil) of your soul and destiny, will rally as many offended people together that he can, along with those full of envy, to secretly gather against you. This is why dreamers and visionaries must spend as much time praying, as they do dreaming! I always ask the Lord to ambush the ambushes of the enemy! However, here is the good news; God's got your back! When you walk in faith and integrity, God will protect and deliver you.

Even though Joseph's brothers conspired to kill him, God's grace and mercy showed up. His brothers had already put him in a pit with the plan to kill him. Instead, God used his brother Reuben to protect his life. Yes, they sold him into slavery for a profit, but God preserved his life. Envy can be a deadly thing. Don't underestimate those who are envious.

...but who is able to stand before envy?
Proverbs 27:4

Envy is an
insidious motivator.

Envy is a work of the flesh. **Galatians 5:21.** Not only does it assault others, it attacks the health of its possessor! **Proverbs 14:30.** Envy is an insidious motivator. It was envy that moved Joseph's brothers to sell him into slavery.

> **And the patriarchs, moved with envy, sold Joseph into Egypt: but God was with him.**
>
> **Acts 7:9**

It was envy that moved Joseph's brothers to sell him into slavery.

Jesus Christ himself knew he was delivered to Pilate to be crucified because of envy! **Matthew 27:18.** The Apostle Paul also experienced attacks in his Ministry because of envy. **Acts 13:45.** Even religious people, and people in your same ethnic group, will persecute you because of envy. They envied Paul because of his success (they saw the multitudes).

> **For he [Jesus] knew that for envy they had delivered him.**
>
> **Matthew 27:18**

But when the Jews saw the multitudes, they were filled with envy, and spake against those things which were spoken by Paul, contradicting and blaspheming.

Acts 13:45

Envy is not something that only the lesser has towards the greater. Sometimes people that have obvious success will hinder, block opportunities, and dilute the success of those whose ministries seem to be far less successful in the eyes of man. Sometimes this is done overtly, and sometimes covertly! In times of relationship challenges, how many times have leaders and ministers said to themselves, "Why would they do that? It just does not make any sense!" The spirit of envy does not make sense, it makes trouble!

The spirit of envy does not make sense, it makes trouble!

Some indeed preach Christ even of envy and strife; and some also of good will:

Philippians 1:15

Some people, who were never called, and never even expressed a desire to preach the gospel, will leave your church or business, and start their own, because of offense and envy. That's right, some will even preach the gospel out of envy! Envy is a powerful motivator! It will cause you to do things that you would not ordinarily do. Envy is destructive and hurtful. Don't allow it to enter into your heart. Envy is often the root of unexplained attacks on your life, ministry, and business. When you face envy, continue to walk in faith and integrity. Maintain a "sent" attitude.

> **People with integrity of character do what is right, even when they are being done wrong!**

Integrity, the Dreamer's Protector

Joseph was a man of integrity. In the midst of all the adversity, trouble, and wrong done to him, Joseph walked uprightly before the Lord. People with integrity of character do what is right, even when they are being done wrong! Integrity is moral soundness or purity; incorruptness; uprightness; honesty. Integrity comes from the word "integer." Wholeness in moral character is an integral part of integrity.

Joseph was sold into slavery by his very own brothers, because of envy. One might expect him to become a very bitter, defensive, or mean spirited person. However,

Joseph's integrity of character brought him to a place of trust with the very person who held him in captivity. Potiphar recognized Joseph's integrity and placed him over his entire household. Even though you have authority over someone's life, it does not mean that you can trust them! However, Potiphar found that he could trust Joseph. Even though Joseph was wrongfully enslaved, he worked diligently for his master, and God caused all the works of his hands to prosper. Not only will integrity preserve you, it sets the platform for God to prosper you!

And he left all that he had in Joseph's hand; and he knew not ought he had, save the bread which he did eat. And Joseph was a goodly person and well favoured.

Genesis 39:6

Potiphar trusted Joseph's character so much that he put all that he had in Joseph's hand. He only concerned himself with what was needed at the time. Joseph is making the best of a bad situation. He is sold into slavery, walking in his integrity, and experiencing God's blessing. As I said before, Potiphar's wife took a liking to Joseph, and wanted to have sexual relations with him.

And it came to past after these things, that his master's wife cast her eyes upon Joseph; and she said, Lie with me.

Genesis 39:7

Joseph, being a man of integrity, refused her offer! Joseph understood he was in a trusted position and that it was wrong to commit adultery, no matter what wrong was done to him. In fact, Joseph saw such an act as a sin against God, not just a betrayal of man!

But he refused, and said unto his master's wife, Behold, my master wotteth not what is with me in the house, and he hath committed all that he hath to my hand;

There is none greater in this house than I; neither hath he kept back anything from me but thee, because thou art his wife: how then can I do this great wickedness, and sin against God?

Genesis 39:8-9

Again, Joseph was more interested in pleasing God than Potiphar's wife or himself. His integrity of character refused to be corrupted by the advances of Potiphar's wife. Joseph was determined to walk uprightly before God. He was determined to maintain his moral integrity and purity. Like Joseph, we must be determined to maintain moral soundness, because lust does not take no for an answer. Potiphar's wife kept after him to sleep with her. And we thought sexual harassment is a modern day issue! She harassed him daily.

Chapter 2

And it came to pass, as she spake to Joseph day by day, that he hearkened not unto her, to lie by her or be with her.

Genesis 39:10

Be forewarned my brothers and sisters, lust is a powerful force! Even if you are a Christian, you must guard yourself, and not allow yourself to be put in a position where it becomes easier to commit sexual sin. Joseph didn't wait for Potiphar and all the servants to leave the house, and then decide to go and clean Potiphar's bedroom! If you have an unhealthy attraction towards a member of the opposite sex, don't allow yourself to be left alone with them. Not only did Joseph refuse to have sex with her, he also avoided being in her presence as much as possible.

And it came to pass about this time, that Joseph went into the house to do his business; and there where none of the men of the house there within. And she caught him by his garment, saying, Lie with me: and he left his garment in her hand, and fled, and got him out.

Genesis 39:11-12

Sometimes people think they can control their own sexual desires or handle the sexual advances of others. If you ever find yourself in this situation, I recommend the

Joseph method. Get the heck out of there! He left his clothes in her hand and fled. He didn't jump spiritual, and ask her to kneel and pray with him, that this desire might pass. No, he just got out of "Dodge!" Joseph was not being weak, he was being wise. Besides, his response was scriptural. The Bible does say flee fornication! **1 Corinthians 6:18.**

Because Joseph rejected Potiphar's wife's sexual advances, she falsely accused him of sexual assault. Potiphar put Joseph in prison.

And it came to pass, when his master heard the words of his wife, which she spake unto him, saying, After his manner did thy servant to me; that his wrath was kindled. And Joseph's master took him, and put him into the prison, a place where the king's prisoners were bound: and he was there in the prison.

Genesis 39:19-20

I believe it was Joseph's integrity that protected him from Potiphar's wrath. Yes, Joseph was put in prison but he could have easily been killed because of Potiphar's anger. Joseph refused to "sin against God!" He walked uprightly before God, and therefore God was able to justly protect his life!

Even though Joseph was put in prison, the LORD showed him mercy and gave him favor with the keeper of the prison. Ultimately, Joseph's prison experience led to his exaltation and the fulfillment of his God-given dream! As you pursue your God-given dream and destiny, walk uprightly before God, and let integrity guide you.

The integrity of the upright shall guide them: but the perverseness of transgressors shall destroy them.

Proverbs 11:3

Like Joseph, Abimelech also discovered that integrity is the dreamer's protector, when he encountered Abraham. As Abraham took his journey of faith, when he came to Ge'rar, he told Abimelech that Sarah his wife was his sister. Abraham did this for fear that Abimelech would kill him for his wife Sarah. Sure enough, Abimelech took Sarah thinking she was just Abraham's sister. God came to Abimelech in a dream and warned him about his intention to take Sarah for himself. God told him he would be put to death if he touched another man's wife. Abimelech then explained to God that Abraham had lied to him and said Sarah was his sister.

Said he not unto me, She is my sister? and she, even herself said, He is my brother: in the integrity of my heart and the innocency of my hands have I done this. And God said in a dream, Yea, I know that thou didst this in the integrity of thy heart; for I also withheld thee

**from sinning against me: therefore suffered I
thee not to touch her.**

Genesis 20:5-6

Integrity of heart
does not mean you
never make a mistake.

Abimelech had made a mistake, and was about to sin against God, based on false information. He had made a mistake in the integrity of his heart! Integrity of heart does not mean you never make a mistake. It does mean however that you walk uprightly according to the information you do have. People with integrity of heart will admit and correct their mistakes when they have the truth or correct information. More importantly, integrity will protect you.

God told Abimelech He knew he had acted in the integrity of his heart. God protected Abimelech by keeping him from touching Sarah, and sinning against God! Integrity is the dreamer's protector. God knows if we're acting in integrity when we make mistakes, or just trying to be slick, and hood-wink someone! No one likes to make mistakes, but thanks be to God, that those mistakes made in integrity of heart afford us God's protection.

Walking in integrity can keep your mistakes from turning into sin! When you walk in integrity, God will keep you from walking further out of His will because of misinformation. I believe people who lack integrity, and knowingly disobey God, will forfeit His divine intervention, and protection in their lives.

> **When you walk in integrity, God will keep you from walking further out of His will because of misinformation.**

Favor, the Dreamer's Power

God-given dreams and visions always require abilities and resources that are greater than our own. In short, God-given dreams and visions require God-given power to bring them to pass! No matter how grand the dream or vision; no matter how gifted, talented, educated, wealthy, or physically strong you are, you will need the help of others to bring the dream or vision to pass. God will give you favor with key people who will support, defend, and promote you, and your cause. Favor causes people to have a kind regard towards us. God-given favor gives us an advantage for success!

God-given favor gives us an advantage for success!

God gives us favor for our good and His purposes. Walking in the favor of God does not mean that life will always be smooth sailing. Like Joseph, you may find yourself in the most difficult of circumstances. However, the favor of God will eventually position you for more favorable circumstances, as you walk in integrity, and obedience to God!

God gives us favor for our good and His purposes.

Joseph was sold into slavery and ended up in Potiphar's house, an officer of Pharaoh. **See Genesis chapter 39.** The Bible says God was with Joseph and he became a prosperous man, even as a slave in his master's house. Joseph's master, Potiphar, saw that the Lord was with Joseph, to the point that everything he did prospered. Therefore, Potiphar promoted Joseph to overseer over his house. The word of God tells us that Joseph was "well favored" in his master's house.

And he left all that he had in Joseph's hand; and he knew not ought he had, save the bread which he did eat. And Joseph was a goodly person, and well favoured.

Genesis 39:6

After Potiphar's wife falsely accused Joseph of attempted sexual assault, Joseph was thrown into prison. Once again, even in the midst of imprisonment, God gave Joseph favor with the keeper of the prison.

But the Lord was with Joseph, and shewed him mercy, and gave him favour in the sight of the keeper of the prison.

Genesis 39:21

Learn to look for the favor of God!

Joseph ended up running things in the prison, for the keeper of the prison, just as he did when he was in Potiphar's house. Learn to look for the favor of God! Learn to follow the favor! Sometimes we can get so focused on our hardships, that we don't recognize God's favor. God had a plan and a purpose for Joseph's life. God had given him a dream. When it looked like Joseph had no power to advance his life and dream, God's favor showed up on the scene! Favor is God's power to advance your God-given dreams and visions!

> ## Favor is God's power to advance your God-given dreams and visions!

Favor is influence and influence is power! Influence is the power to persuade, effect, and move. Influence is spiritual power, moral power, and physical power. The influence of the Holy Spirit working in us and through us is spiritual power. The influence of the word of God (the Ten Commandments) working in us and through us is moral power. The influence of our health, wealth, and resources, for the Church of Jesus Christ, and the Kingdom of God is physical power.

Believers must learn to be courageous, and use their faith to influence the world for righteousness. Influence is not neutral! Neutrality will not advance you, or the cause of

Christ! If you want to move your vehicle forward, you must put it in a forward gear. If you want it to move backward, you put it in reverse gear. However, to put the vehicle in neutral, is to disengage the active gears, and put it in a passive gear. Now the vehicle is susceptible to any force, from any direction! In neutral, the vehicle is powerless to move itself forward or resist any outside force.

Sometimes when believers are driving down the road of faith, and encounter a difficult spiritual, moral, or physical decision, they try to play it safe, and just put their faith in neutral. They keep their mouths shut instead of speaking up and out (against or for), concerning the controversial issues of the day. They don't want to offend the "politically correct," or incur the persecution of the ungodly. This sometimes comes in the form of peer pressure. Consequently, these ungodly forces are able to adversely affect their lives, because of the passive gear they allowed themselves to fall into!

> **To remain neutral in the use of your influence, is to surrender your spiritual, moral, and physical power to your enemy.**

Let us be the salt of the earth and the light of the world. We must engage our courage and faith, and use our influence to advance the "kingdom of God." To remain neutral in the use of your influence, is to surrender your spiritual, moral, and physical power to your enemy. Don't allow your adversaries, circumstances, or hardships to intimidate you! God has not given us a spirit of fear.

> **But the favor of God can come on you, that will allow you to engage a supernatural gear in the spirit, and catapult you out of that place of problem, into a place of promotion.**

Like Joseph, we as believers may sometimes find ourselves in situations or circumstances that seem to have stripped us of our ability to free ourselves, change our condition, and move forward toward our dreams and visions. But the favor of God can come on you, that will allow you to engage a supernatural gear in the spirit, and catapult you out of that place of problem, into a place of promotion. Joseph went from the prison to the palace, because of the favor of God.

The presence of problems does not mean the absence of God's favor. Sometimes people become so focused on their problems and hardships that they can't recognize the presence of God's favor. Their attitude is such that they see themselves as being "sold" (in bondage) to their circumstances. If you are unable to see the favor of God in your life or situation, perhaps it is time for a new attitude!

The Authority of Favor

Favor releases a certain authority into your life! Authority is the right to influence. To help us understand and grab hold to the authority of favor, I want to cast favor alongside credibility and character. Credibility says you really have a call, gift, anointing, experience or expertise. Character says you have integrity, morality, you are faithful, loving, and obedient. Favor says God is with you. Credibility gets people to listen to you; Character gets people to trust you; and favor gets people to do for you.

Favor releases a certain authority into your life!

When Joseph was sold into slavery to Potiphar, he was placed over Potiphar's entire household. Joseph obviously had some genuine administrative ability [credibility] to run Potiphar's house. After Joseph was falsely accused of sexual assault, by Potiphar's wife, and cast into prison, he once again, was promoted to a place of authority. He was put over the entire prison, by the keeper of the prison. Joseph had a genuine gift to interpret dreams as experienced by Pharaoh's butler and baker, whom were put into prison with Joseph, because they had fallen out of favor with Pharaoh. It was the butler, that eventually told Pharaoh about Joseph's credibility to interpret dreams. While Joseph was over Potiphar's house, the Bible says Potiphar did not know or concern himself with any of the household responsibilities, because he trusted Joseph [character]. Apparently, so did the keeper of the prison. Usually, you don't place the prisoner over the prison! Potiphar, the keeper of the Prison, Pharaoh's butler, and Pharaoh himself, did things for Joseph that Joseph could not do for himself [favor]. They all promoted him to a place of authority, or were instrumental in Joseph's promotion in the case of Pharaoh's butler. The favor on Joseph's life got them all to do things for Joseph, that ultimately resulted in him reaching and fulfilling his God-given dream and vision.

And Joseph was brought down to Egypt; and Potiphar, an officer of Pharaoh, captain of the guard, an Egyptian, bought him of the hands of the Ishmeelites, which had brought him down thither. And the LORD was with Joseph, and he was a prosperous man; and he was in the house of his master the Egyptian. And his master saw that the LORD *was* with him, and

that the LORD made all that he did to prosper in his hand. And Joseph found grace in his sight, and he served him: and he made him overseer over his house, and all *that* he had he put into his hand. And it came to pass from the time *that* he had made him overseer in his house, and over all that he had, that the LORD blessed the Egyptian's house for Joseph's sake; and the blessing of the LORD was upon all that he had in the house, and in the field. And he left all that he had in Joseph's hand; and he knew not ought he had, save the bread which he did eat. And Joseph was *a* goodly *person*, and well favoured.

Genesis 39:1-6

Then spake the chief butler unto Pharaoh, saying, I do remember my faults this day: Pharaoh was wroth with his servants, and put me in ward in the captain of the guard's house, *both* me and the chief baker: And we dreamed a dream in one night, I and he; we dreamed each man according to the interpretation of his dream. And *there was* there with us a young man, an Hebrew, servant to the captain of the guard; and we told him, and he interpreted to us our dreams; to each man according to his dream he did interpret. And it came to pass, as he interpreted to us, so it was; me he restored unto mine office, and him he hanged. Then Pharaoh sent and called Joseph, and they brought him hastily out of the dungeon: and he shaved *himself*, and changed his raiment, and came in unto Pharaoh. And Pharaoh said unto Joseph, I have dreamed a dream, and *there is* none that can interpret it: and I have heard say of thee, *that* thou canst understand a dream to interpret it. And Joseph answered Pharaoh, saying, *It is* not in me: God shall give Pharaoh an answer of peace.

Genesis 41:9-16

And the patriarchs, moved with envy, sold Joseph into Egypt: but God was with him, And delivered him out of all his afflictions, and gave him favour and wisdom in the sight of Pharaoh king of Egypt; and he made him governor over Egypt and all his house.

Acts 7:9-10

Chapter 3

JOSEPH'S SENT ATTITUDE

At the latter part of Joseph's life when his dream had come into manifestation, Joseph had become everything his dream had prophesied. Joseph had accomplished great things with God. He was now that exalted leader. God had so promoted Joseph that he was second in command in Egypt. Only Pharaoh was greater. After experiencing many trials and tribulations, the word of God reveals Joseph's attitude. His own brothers had mistreated him and sold him into slavery. Now at a time when his brothers needed his help, Joseph's brothers had to come to him in Egypt, and asked for his help during a time of famine. Joseph reminded his brothers that they sold him into slavery and to Egypt, but God sent him to Egypt to preserve life.

Now therefore be not grieved, nor angry with yourselves, that you sold me hither: for God did send me before you to preserve life. And _GOD SENT ME_ [my emphasis] before you to preserve you a posterity in the earth, and to save your lives by a great deliverance. So now it was not you that sent me hither, but God: and he has made me a father to Pharaoh, and lord of all his house, and a ruler throughout all the land of Egypt.

Genesis 45:5, 7-8

**Joseph's attitude
was that he was
"sent," and not "sold."**

Wow! Joseph's attitude was that he was "sent," and not "sold." After all the hardship, difficulties, obstacles, setbacks, and injustices he had experienced, Joseph had not grown to be some bitter old man. Looking back on those difficult times in his life, he saw himself as being "sent" by God, and not just "sold" by man.

> **Joseph had refused to develop a "sold" mentality! Joseph refused to see himself as being "sold" to his circumstances.**

Joseph had refused to develop a "sold" mentality! Joseph refused to see himself as being "sold" to his circumstances. His attitude was that he was "sent" by God and not in bondage to his circumstances! Don't allow your circumstances to dictate what your attitude will be. Let the word of God and your God-given dream or vision inspire you to a "sent" attitude. I'm not suggesting that Joseph went about life (24/7) showing all thirty-two of his teeth. No, it is obvious that he went through some bad times. I'm just saying, you can go through bad times with a good attitude!

> **I'm just saying, you can go through bad times with a good attitude!**

In fact, that's how you get through bad times successfully: by having a good (sent) attitude. You don't have to be in bondage to your circumstances. Don't allow yourself to have an "I am sold" mind-set. Sometime during his trials and tribulations Joseph resolved the "Dreamer's Dilemma."

God Is With Me

Joseph had a God-given dream and vision in his heart. He was rejected by his brothers, and sold into slavery; twice! His father thought he was dead, and Joseph found himself alone, in bondage, in a strange country. Yet, he was conscious of God's presence, and believed God was still with him. When Potiphar's wife tried to seduce Joseph, he said "...how then can I do this great wickedness, and sin against God?" **Genesis 39:9.**

While in prison on trumped-up charges, Joseph interpreted a dream for Pharaoh's butler and his baker, whom had fallen out of favor with Pharaoh. He told them interpretations belong to God, and then exercised his faith to give the interpretation from God. **Genesis 40:8.** Even though he was imprisoned, Joseph still believed God was with him, and would give him the interpretation. He was willing to use his gifts and talents for the benefit of others, even in the midst of personal adversity.

Like Joseph, we must get to a point where we believe God is with us. Even when things are difficult and people have rejected us, we must believe that God will never leave us nor forsake us as His children.

Let your conversation be without covetousness; and be content with such

**things as ye have: for he hath said, I will never
leave thee, nor forsake thee.**

Hebrews 13:5

God is faithful. God is greater than your circumstance
and your adversary. Don't fear. God is good, and He has a
willingness to help you. You must trust Him, and have a
"sent" attitude, which says, "God is with me!"

God Will Deliver Me

Joseph had an expectation that God would deliver him
out of slavery and imprisonment. He never lost hope. He had
a "sent" by God attitude. After he interpreted the butler's
dream, he told the butler to remember him when Pharaoh
restored him to chief butler. Joseph told the butler to mention
him to Pharaoh, and get him out of prison, because he was
innocent. Again, Joseph expected God to deliver him.
Joseph expected the favor of God to be in manifestation in
his life and situation. He expected favor with the chief butler,
and favor with Pharaoh.

**But think on me when it shall be well with thee,
and shew kindness I pray thee, unto me, and
make mention of me unto Pharaoh, and bring
me out of this house: For indeed I was stolen
away out of the land of the Hebrews: and here**

**also have I done nothing that they should put
me into the dungeon.**

Genesis 40:14-15

After Joseph interpreted the butler's dream, and he was
restored to his position of chief butler, he forgot about
Joseph. In fact, Joseph sat in prison for two full years after
his encounter with Pharaoh's butler. One day Pharaoh
dreamed a dream, slept again and dreamed another dream.
His dreams troubled his spirit, so he called on all the
magicians of Egypt, and all the wise men to interpret his
dreams, but they could not. Then the chief butler
remembered Joseph and told Pharaoh about him.

**Then spake the chief butler unto Pharaoh,
saying, I do remember my faults this day:
Pharaoh was wroth with his servants, and put
me in ward in the captain of the guard's house,
both me and the chief baker: And we dreamed
a dream in one night, I and he; we dreamed
each man according to the interpretation of his
dream. And there was there with us a young
man, an Hebrew, servant to the captain of the
guard; and we told him, and he interpreted to
us our dreams; to each man according to his
dream he did interpret. And it came to pass, as
he interpreted to us, so it was; me he restored
unto mine office, and him he hanged. Then**

Pharaoh sent and called Joseph, and they brought him hastily out of the dungeon: and he shaved himself, and changed his raiment, and came in unto Pharaoh.

Genesis 41:9-14

Pharaoh told Joseph he dreamed a dream that none could interpret, but he heard Joseph had the ability to interpret dreams. Joseph responded by telling Pharaoh God would give him an answer to his dreams, and it would bring peace to his heart. Joseph spoke his faith, even before he heard Pharaoh's dreams. Pharaoh told Joseph his dreams and he interpreted them. Pharaoh was so impressed with Joseph's gift to interpret dreams that he promoted him to second in command over Egypt. God had delivered Joseph out of slavery, and prison, and promoted him to a leadership position, second only to Pharaoh himself. God knows how to deliver His people!

The Lord knoweth how to deliver the godly out of temptations, and to reserve the unjust unto the day of judgment to be punished:

2 Peter 2:9

Praise God! No matter what situation or circumstance you may find yourself in, God knows how to rescue you. God is not against you but for you. God sent Jesus to help us, not hurt us. God is good and His mercy endures forever. Walk in faith, and integrity, and expect God to deliver you.

God Gives Me Favor

From the study of the life of the patriarch Joseph, it is clear that God gave him favor. Joseph had a conviction that God was with him, despite the difficult times he experienced. As believers, we too can have the same conviction. Favor is a major component of the grace of God. Grace is often defined as God's unmerited favor. The word of God tells us we are saved by grace through faith.

For by grace are you ye saved through faith: and that not of yourselves; it is the gift of God: Not of works, lest any man should boast.
Ephesians 2:8-9

God saved us, not because of our good works, but because of His grace. He loves us, and sent His Son Jesus to die for us (our sins), on the cross. God saved us according to His good pleasure. The grace or favor of God says, I am for you; My will is blessing and good for your life; I am leaning towards you to help you. Not only should we exercise our faith for the grace and favor of God, we should celebrate His grace (give praise to the glory of his grace).

Having predestinated us unto the adoption of children by Jesus Christ to himself, according

to the good pleasure of his will, To the praise of the glory of his grace, wherein he hath made us accepted in the beloved.

Ephesians 1:5-6

> **We tap into
> the grace
> or unmerited
> favor of God
> through our
> faith in God.**

We tap into the grace or unmerited favor of God through our faith in God. As you pursue your dreams and visions, don't allow hard times, rejection, obstacles, or persecution from your adversary stop you, and steal or dilute your faith in the grace and favor of God. Believe that God favors you! You must develop a conviction that God favors you as His child. It is a good confession to say daily, "God favors me!" Remember, to talk about the grace of God, is to talk about the favor of God. God wants us to have this conviction of faith. He tells us to come boldly to the throne of grace to get the help we need.

Let us therefore come boldly unto the throne
of grace, that we may obtain mercy, and find
grace to help in time of need.

Hebrews 4:16

Again, to speak of the grace of God is to speak of the favor of God. In fact, grace is the exercise of love, kindness, favor, and mercy. It's vital to grab ahold to the grace, favor, and mercy connection. Grace is enjoyment of divine favor! In manifestation, mercy flows from God's grace. In God's favor (grace) he has mercy on us!

...for in my wrath I smote thee, but in my favour have I had mercy on thee.

Isaiah 60:10

Perhaps like Joseph, you too find yourself in a situation or circumstances beyond your natural ability to overcome. Nevertheless, child of God, God is with you. Expect God's favor and mercy to be manifest in your life. Joseph was falsely accused, and put in prison, but the word of God says, God showed him mercy and gave him favor. Where there is grace, there is favor and mercy!

But the LORD was with Joseph, and showed him mercy, and gave him favour in the sight of the keeper of the prison.

Genesis 39:21

The Bible says we are saved by grace through faith. Grace yields its power (love, kindness, favor, and mercy) to faith, and faith partakes of the benefits of God's grace. A "sent" attitude requires faith in God. People with a "sent" attitude have a conviction that God's favor, and mercy, will be manifest in the midst of their circumstances.

Chapter 3

God Will Give Me Wisdom

A core conviction of those with a "sent" attitude is that God will give them the wisdom they need to endure, and overcome their trials and tribulations. People with a "sent" attitude will have joy even in the midst of unfavorable circumstances. Joy is an attitude indicator! To have joy in the midst of your difficult circumstances you must know something! This is not just head knowledge, but also heart knowledge.

My brethren, count it all joy when ye fall into divers temptations; Knowing this, that the trying of your faith worketh patience. But let patience have her perfect work, that ye may be perfect and entire, wanting nothing.

James 1:2-4

Having joy in our troubles and hardships is an indicator of our spiritual maturity and faith in God. This joy is not based on our emotions or comfort, neither the pressures we feel from external circumstances. Rather, it is based on the knowledge, that God is with us, and developing the virtues of patience, and perseverance in us. Also, that God will give us wisdom to pass the tests, trials, and tribulations of life! This joy is based on the knowledge, and belief, that God is bringing us to a place of spiritual maturity. It is joy that recognizes and cooperates with God's processes in life.

SENT OR SOLD: THE DREAMER'S DILEMMA

The word of God also reveals to us, that God's wisdom is available to us, as we go through tough times. In fact, it tells us to ask God for wisdom, when we face difficult circumstances that we don't know how to navigate, and come out on top. It's important to understand God is willing to give us the wisdom we need to win in life. God will give His wisdom freely to all who ask in faith. However, we must ask in faith and not waver. We must believe that God has answered our prayer for wisdom, when we pray, even though the circumstances have not changed in the natural.

If any of you lack wisdom, let him ask of God, that giveth to all men liberally, and upbraideth not; and it shall be given him. But let him ask in faith, nothing wavering. For he that wavereth is like a wave of the sea driven with the wind and tossed. For let not that man think that he shall receive any thing of the Lord. A double minded man is unstable in all his ways.

James 1:5-8

Joseph found himself in some very unpleasant circumstances, even though he held a God-given dream in his heart. Joseph's brothers envied him because of his dreams, put him in a pit, and sold him into slavery. Joseph was sold into slavery not once, but twice, and also put in prison on false charges of sexual misconduct. He ended up ultimately in the palace, in an exalted position as a leader.

The Bible tells us that God gave Joseph wisdom among other things, to empower him to navigate the pit, prison, and ultimately the palace.

And the patriarchs, moved with envy, sold Joseph into Egypt: but God was with him, And delivered him out of all his afflictions, and gave him favour and wisdom in the sight of Pharaoh king of Egypt; and he made him governor over Egypt and all his house.

Acts 7:9-10

It was the wisdom that God gave Joseph to interpret dreams ,that brought Joseph before Pharaoh. Pharaoh had those troubling dreams, in which none of the magicians, or wise men of Egypt could interpret. Joseph had already operated in the wisdom to interpret dreams while in prison. He had given the interpretation of the dreams of Pharaoh's baker, and chief butler, whom had fallen out of favor with Pharaoh. Just as Joseph declared, the baker was killed, and the chief butler was restored according to Joseph's interpretation. The butler remembered Joseph's ability to interpret dreams, and informed Pharaoh. Pharaoh then called for Joseph out of prison and told Joseph his dreams. Before Joseph even heard Pharaoh's dreams, he believed God would give him the wisdom to interpret the dreams. Again, people with a "sent" attitude have the conviction, "God will give me wisdom!"

Again, people with a "sent" attitude have the conviction, "God will give me wisdom!"

And Joseph answered Pharaoh, saying, it is not in me: God shall give Pharaoh an answer of peace.

Genesis 41:16

Pharaoh recognized the wisdom God had given Joseph, which resulted in the exaltation of Joseph as second in command to Pharaoh. God gave Joseph the wisdom to take him all the way to a leadership position in the palace; with a few stops in the pit, Potiphar's house, and the prison!

And Pharaoh said unto his servants, Can we find such a one as this is, a man in whom the Spirit of God is? And Pharaoh said unto Joseph, Forasmuch as God hath showed thee all this, there is none so discreet and wise as thou art: Thou shalt be over my house, and according unto thy word shall all my people be ruled: only in the throne will I be greater than thou. And Pharaoh said unto Joseph, See, I have set thee over all the land of Egypt. And

Pharaoh took off his ring from his hand, and put it upon Joseph's hand, and arrayed him in vestures of fine linen, and put a gold chain about his neck; And he made him to ride in the second chariot which he had; and they cried before him, Bow the knee: and he made him ruler over all the land of Egypt. And Pharaoh said unto Joseph, I am Pharaoh, and without thee shall no man lift up his hand or foot in all the land of Egypt.

Genesis 41:38-44

Wisdom is knowledge guided by understanding. It is the skillful application of the knowledge of God in everyday living. Many times people ask God for wisdom, but don't always recognize the wisdom of God. Let me give you a biblical description of wisdom. Wisdom is spiritual in nature, moral in character, and practical in its application.

Wisdom is spiritual in nature. Wisdom goes beyond intelligence or mental abilities. While I am all for a college education, wisdom does not come from a college education. I'm talking about the wisdom of God. Wisdom comes from God! God gives us wisdom through the Spirit!

As for these four children, God gave them knowledge and skill in all learning and

wisdom: and Daniel had understanding in all visions and dreams.

Daniel 1:17

Wisdom crieth without; she uttereth her voice in the streets: She crieth in the chief place of concourse, in the openings of the gates: in the city she uttereth her words, saying, How long, ye simple ones, will ye love simplicity? and the scorners delight in their scorning, and fools hate knowledge? Turn you at my reproof: behold, _I will pour out my spirit unto you_ [my emphasis], I will make known my words unto you.

Proverbs 1:20-23

Wisdom is moral in character. It is vital to recognize the moral aspect of wisdom. People tend to think that wisdom is just being shrewd in business, and winning at all costs. When I was growing up as a teenager in the latter 1960's to early 1970's, there was a common saying among the "homeboys" in the hood concerning the success of a hustle. We would say, "Man, they are getting over like a fat rat in a cheese factory!" In other words, hook-or-crook, someone was experiencing a degree of success in their schemes. However, true wisdom has a moral component. True wisdom will not lead you to lie, cheat, and steal to prosper in life. We know this because the word of God says the fear of the Lord is the beginning of wisdom. The fear of the Lord is reverence, respect, honor, and awe of God. The fear of the Lord is the starting point of wisdom. So if the thing you are about to do does not reverence, respect, or bring honor to God, it is not the wisdom of God.

> **The fear of the LORD is the beginning of wisdom: and the knowledge of the holy is understanding.**
>
> **Proverbs 9:10**

> **The fear of the LORD is the beginning of wisdom: a good understanding have all they that do his commandments: his praise endureth for ever.**
>
> **Psalm 111:10**

The fear of the Lord is not some mysterious quality that only a few are privy to. No, it is a choice we make. We must choose to be moral in life. We must choose to operate according to the commandments of God. We must choose the fear of the Lord in life, and in any given situation or circumstance.

> **For that they hated knowledge, and did not choose the fear of the LORD: They would none of my counsel: they despised all my reproof.**
>
> **Proverbs 1:29-30**

The wisdom of God is practical in its application. Often when people think of wisdom, and a wise person, they envision some elderly man living in an isolated environment, with a long gray beard espousing nebulous sayings. However, godly wisdom is practical in its application. In other words, the wisdom of God is useful and usable in everyday living. The basis or theory behind the wisdom of a thing may be very complicated, but on the working end, it is practical and executable. God designed and created our bodies in all its systems and organs, yet as a whole in our operation in this world, our bodies are very practical. To govern and lead people, require the application of wisdom in a practical manner. God designed and created the solar systems. Obviously, these systems are very complicated, yet as far as our survival, and interaction with them, their design is very practical. The wisdom of God puts a handle on the cup of complicated things (theories, laws, principles and ideas) in life, so we can grab hold to them, and use them in everyday living!

By me kings reign, and princes decree justice. By me princes rule, and nobles, even all the judges of the earth.

Proverbs 8:15

Chapter 4

AN ATTITUDE OF HOPE

Dreams and visions inspire us. They give us hope, especially God-given dreams and visions. Joseph's dream inspired hope in his life. Joseph's "sent" attitude reflected his hope in God.

Joseph's "sent" attitude reflected his hope in God.

Hope is a vital force in life, particularly during difficult times. Joseph was put in a pit, sold into slavery, falsely accused, and put into prison; but he never lost sight of his dream! Hope is a force that empowers us to move forward in life! While faith equips us to live confidently in the present without the manifestations of favorable conditions, hope looks to the future, and motivates us to keep moving forward in life, in spite of hardships and obstacles. Faith is present tense, but hope is future tense. The Bible says faith is the substance of things hoped for.

**Hope is a
force that
empowers
us to move
forward in life!**

**Now faith is the substance of things hoped for,
the evidence of things not seen.**

Hebrews 11:1

People who have hope, look forward to the future. People who do not have hope, look fearfully to the future. Many people are without hope in the world today. They are anchored down and drowning in a cesspool of fear, immorality, crime, war, and economic disaster. Like Joseph, people who trust in God are a people of hope. God is the source of true hope. In fact, the Bible says God is the God of hope.

**Now the God of hope fill you with all joy and
peace in believing, that ye may abound in
hope, through the power of the Holy Ghost.**

Romans 15:13

Chapter 4

Hope is expectation of future good! Hope is more than desire. Bible hope is a confident expectation of future good. David said his hope (confident expectation) was from God.

My soul, wait thou only upon God; for my expectation is from him.

Psalm 62:5

People with a "sent" attitude understand the connection between hope and promise. Hope is the confident expectation of fulfillment of promise. Hope has its roots in the promises (word) of God. At this point, we must ask ourselves, What is a promise? Simply put, a promise is a reason to expect something. To expect means: to look forward to; to anticipate the coming or occurrence of; to wait for.

To illustrate, the power of hope on our attitude can easily be seen in the promise made to a young child concerning that special toy, or electronic device they desire for Christmas. Christmas can be two months away (seemingly a life-time for a young child!), but once a parent makes that child a promise to give it to them, hope springs alive, and a different attitude comes forth. In other words, their new attitude reflects their new hope.

God has given us many precious promises in the Bible. Therefore, we should be a people of hope, because we are a people of promise. If we believe what the word of God says about God's character, and ability to do whatever He has promised, we become a people of hope.

> **Grace and peace be multiplied unto you through the knowledge of God, and of Jesus our Lord, According as his divine power hath given unto us all things that pertain unto life and godliness, through the knowledge of him that hath called us to glory and virtue: Whereby are given unto us exceeding great and precious promises: that by these ye might be partakers of the divine nature, having escaped the corruption that is in the world through lust.**
>
> **2 Peter 1:2-4**

Where there is promise, there is the potential for hope! We have hope for life beyond the grave, because God promises all believers in Jesus Christ eternal life.

> **Paul, a servant of God, and an apostle of Jesus Christ, according to the faith of God's elect, and the acknowledging of the truth which is after godliness; In hope of eternal life, which God, that cannot lie, promised before the world began;**
>
> **Titus 1-2**

Chapter 4

Sometimes people will persecute you because of your hope in God's promises. That's true! I know it sounds crazy, but some people will actually come against you because of your hope in the promises of God. Some are just pessimistic in nature, and don't like being around optimistic people. Others become angry, because your hope and faith in the promises of God shines a light on their lack of hope, faith, and understanding of the promises of God. Don't you stop hoping in God. Joseph's brothers hated him because of his dream. Joseph's hopeful attitude, because of his dream, rubbed them the wrong way! Even the apostle Paul was persecuted for his hope in the promise of God.

And now I stand and am judged for the hope of the promise made of God unto our fathers: Unto which promise our twelve tribes, instantly serving God day and night, hope to come. For which hope's sake, king Agrippa, I am accused of the Jews.

Acts 26:6-7

In pursuit of our dream and visions we can face some really discouraging circumstances. Like Abraham, we must hope against hope. In other words, when there was no natural reason for Abraham to hope, he grabbed hold to some supernatural hope from the promise of God. Abraham had no reason to hope for a child born of his very own loins, because of his and Sarah's old age. Hope is a component of faith. Without hope, there can be no faith.

Therefore it is of faith, that it might be by grace; to the end the promise might be sure to all the seed; not to that only which is of the law, but to that also which is of the faith of Abraham; who is the father of us all, (As it is written, I have made thee a father of many nations,) before him whom he believed, even God, who quickeneth the dead, and calleth those things which be not as though they were. Who against hope believed in hope, that he might become the father of many nations, according to that which was spoken, So shall thy seed be. And being not weak in faith, he considered not his own body now dead, when he was about an hundred years old, neither yet the deadness of Sarah's womb: He staggered not at the promise of God through unbelief; but was strong in faith, giving glory to God; And being fully persuaded that, what he had promised, he was able also to perform.

Romans 4:16-21

While faith believes it receives now in the present, hope is that component of faith that empowers us to wait patiently (persevere) until the promise manifests.

For we are saved by hope: but hope that is seen is not hope: for what a man seeth, why doth he yet hope for? But if we hope for that

we see not, then do we with patience wait for
it.

Romans 8:24-25

Are you presently facing a hopeless situation in your life? Like Abraham, do you find yourself in circumstances whereby you must hope against hope? I encourage you to go to the word of God (the Bible) and find a promise from God that answers your problem. Don't give up; don't throw in the towel- hope in God!

Remember the word unto thy servant, upon
which thou hast caused me to hope.

Psalm 119:49

I wait for the LORD, my soul doth wait, and in
his word do I hope.

Psalm 130:5

Perseverance

One of the greatest challenges to dealing with the time element of fulfilling our dreams and visions is the development of patience, and perseverance. The Greek word translated patience in the following scriptures has both the aspects of patience and perseverance.

My brethren, count it all joy when ye fall into
divers temptations: knowing this, that the

trying of your faith worketh patience. But let patience have her perfect work, that ye may be perfect and entire, wanting nothing.

James 1:2-4

And not only so, but we glory in tribulations also, knowing that tribulation worketh patience; And patience, experience; and experience, hope:

Romans 5:3-4

As we study the life of Joseph, you will notice that he had a remarkable attitude in the midst of all his troubles. He maintained a good and joyful spirit. When you have a "sent" attitude, you will have joy even in the face of difficulties and opposition. Having the right attitude in the midst of all the pressures (tribulations) of life, develops patience, and perseverance in us. Patience and perseverance yields the effect of proving, or approval from God. This experience or "effect of proving," produces hope. When you lose hope, your dream dies and your vision is lost. People with a "sent" attitude have a confident expectation that their dreams and visions will come to pass.

Perseverance is a trait that is vital to good character, and fulfilling our dreams, visions, and destiny in Christ. Perseverance can be defined as: The holding to a course of action, belief, or purpose, in spite of difficulties or adversity;

Remaining constant to a purpose, belief, or task, in the face of obstacles or discouragement; to continue moving toward a goal despite difficulties.

Sometimes people confuse perseverance with stubbornness or hard-headedness! I'm not talking about offended, selfish people, who are determined to have things their way no matter what. In fact, some wear their stubbornness as a badge of false righteousness, unwilling to change, or admit they are the cause of most of their troubles. Perseverance is necessary for success in spiritual warfare, particularly in the discipline of prayer.

Praying always with all prayer and supplication in the Spirit, and watching thereunto with all perseverance and supplication for all saints;
Ephesians 6:18

And he spake a parable unto them to this end, that men ought always to pray, and not to faint;
Luke 18:1
Continue in prayer, and watch in the same with thanksgiving;
Colossians 4:2

SENT OR SOLD: THE DREAMER'S DILEMMA

We must persevere through distractions and obstacles that can prevent us from regular communion with the Lord in prayer. We have an alternative to fainting, quitting, or throwing-in-the-towel. To persevere is to endure hardness as a good soldier of the Lord. The apostle Paul pressed (persevered) toward the mark of the high calling of God in Christ. Perseverance is required to reap your harvest. **Galatians 6:9** says we will reap if we faint not. Perseverance is a quality of true love. **1 Corinthians 13:7** tells us that love perseveres. Jacob persevered through Laban's injustice because of his love for Rachel; **Genesis 29:20.** Jesus persevered through the cross to fulfill His assignment from God; **Hebrews 12:2.** Persevere; don't quit before your deliverance (salvation) manifests!

But he that shall endure unto the end, the same shall be saved.
Matthew 24:13

Do you finish what you start? Do you have a history of quitting? People with a "sent" attitude will allow God to build perseverance in their life in the midst of a challenge, or a difficult situation or circumstance. Don't allow yourself to be "sold" under your circumstances. Others should be able to depend on you to carry out your assignment to completion, even when things become difficult. Develop the discipline of daily prayer in your life.

Patience

Again, perseverance and patience, are closely related, so I want to make a distinction between the two. Perseverance focuses on moving forward, and not quitting in the face of hardship, while patience focuses on self-control, and calmness in the face of hardship and delay. Patience can be defined as:The capacity of calm endurance; the capacity of bearing delay and waiting for the right time; the capacity of enduring hardship, delay or inconvenience without complaint, loss of temper, or irritation.

Patience enables us to endure difficult circumstances, without losing self-control, and without becoming bitter towards God or others. Patience empowers us to endure until the manifestation of the promise.

Cast not away therefore your confidence, which hath great recompense of reward. For ye have need of patience, that, after ye have done the will of God, ye might receive the promise.

Hebrews 10:35-36

Patience is a necessary quality to produce the fruit of God's word. Patience (long-suffering) is a fruit of the Spirit.

But that on the good ground are they, which in an honest and good heart, having heard the

word, keep it, and bring forth fruit with
patience.

Luke 8:15

But the fruit of the Spirit is love, joy, peace,
longsuffering, gentleness, goodness, faith,
Meekness, temperance: against such there is
no law.

Galatians 5:22-23

Patience: Is developed through trials and tribulations
[James 1:2-4]; is the product of the scriptures [Romans
14:4-5]; is necessary for soundness of faith [Titus 2:2]; is
indicative of spiritual power [2 Corinthians 12:12]; paves the
way for hope [Romans 5:3-4].

Patience does not become irritable, angry, or grumble
when faced with hardship, inconvenience, or delay.
Perhaps God is building patience in you right now through
the situation you are presently facing. Patient people refuse
to succumb to the instant, microwave, got-to-have-it-now,
culture of this generation. Patient people are willing to suffer
for a season to receive God's best for their life. I believe
Joseph's patience and perseverance were vital qualities of
his "sent" attitude.

Chapter 5

AN ATTITUDE OF FORGIVENESS

I believe people with a "sent" attitude develop and walk in an attitude of forgiveness. Joseph's own brothers had mistreated him to say the least. His brothers were envious of his dreams and vision for his future. They put Joseph in a pit with the intent to kill him. The older brother Rueben talked them out of it, and they ended up selling Joseph into slavery. Joseph was ripped away from the love and comfort of his father, and mother, to a strange place and people. In fact, Joseph was sold, not once, but twice! The second time, he was sold to Potiphar, an officer of Pharaoh's guard. While under Potiphar's authority, God prospered Joseph and he was promoted to overseer of Potiphar's household. Once again, Joseph suffered a major wrong. He was falsely accused of sexual assault by Potiphar's wife. She wanted Joseph to sleep with her, but when he refused, she became angry and made the accusation that landed Joseph in prison. Let you and I be honest, we would most likely have a funky attitude about now, having experienced what Joseph did. At least, I know I would have had to deal with myself concerning my attitude towards those who had done me wrong.

While in prison, Joseph interpreted a dream for Pharaoh's butler and baker, which brought him before Pharaoh himself when he had a disturbing dream. God gave Joseph the wisdom to interpret Pharaohs dream, and Pharaoh promoted Joseph to second in command over all Egypt at that time. Joseph revealed to Pharaoh that God was telling him that seven productive years of grain, would be followed by seven years of famine. God gave Joseph the wisdom to lead the nation of Egypt during this time, and provide sustenance to Egypt, and the surrounding nations, during the seven good years and the seven bad years. When the famine began, Jacob, Joseph's father, heard about the store of grain in Egypt, and sent his sons (Joseph's brothers) to purchase some. When Joseph's brothers got to Egypt, they had to do business with him. However, they did not recognize him, but he knew who they were. With all the wrong done to Joseph by his brothers, one would think that Joseph would have had them killed, or put in prison to say the least. Joseph however, forgave them because of his "sent" attitude. After implementing a scheme that would bring his youngest brother Benjamin and ultimately his father Jacob, and his entire household to Egypt, Joseph revealed himself to his brothers. He was happy to see them, not so he could get revenge, but so that he could bless them!

> And Joseph said unto his brethren, I *am* Joseph; doth my father yet live? And his brethren could not answer him; for they were troubled at his presence. And Joseph said unto his brethren, Come near to me, I pray you. And they came near. And he said, I *am* Joseph your brother, whom ye sold into Egypt. Now therefore be not grieved, nor angry with yourselves, that ye sold me hither: for God did send me before you to preserve life. For these two years *hath* the famine *been* in the land: and yet *there are* five years, in the which *there shall* neither *be* earing nor harvest. And God sent me before you to preserve you a posterity in the earth, and to save your lives by a great deliverance. So now *it was* not you *that* sent me hither, but God: and he hath made me a father to Pharaoh, and lord of all his house, and a ruler throughout all the land of Egypt. Haste ye, and go up to my father, and say unto him, Thus saith thy son Joseph, God hath made me lord of all Egypt: come down unto me, tarry not: And thou shalt dwell in the land of Goshen, and thou shalt be near unto me, thou, and thy

children, and thy children's children, and thy flocks, and thy herds, and all that thou hast: And there will I nourish thee; for yet *there are* five years of famine; lest thou, and thy household, and all that thou hast, come to poverty.

Genesis 45:3-11

Joseph was not bitter with his brothers. His focus was not that his brothers had sold him into slavery, but on the fact that God had sent him to Egypt to be a leader and a deliver. If Joseph had not forgiven his brothers and killed them, he would have destroyed the very purposes for which God had given him so much favor and wisdom to accomplish. Joseph told his brothers that God sent him to Egypt to preserve their lives and their children, not to kill them. After Jacob, Joseph's father died, his brothers became fearful that Joseph would now take revenge on them. However, Joseph was a man of integrity, and walked in an attitude of forgiveness.

And when Joseph's brethren saw that their father was dead, they said, Joseph will peradventure hate us, and will certainly requite us all the evil which we did unto him. And they sent a messenger unto Joseph, saying, Thy father did command before he died, saying, So shall ye say unto Joseph, Forgive, I pray thee now, the trespass of thy brethren, and their

sin; for they did unto thee evil: and now, we pray thee, forgive the trespass of the servants of the God of thy father. And Joseph wept when they spake unto him. And his brethren also went and fell down before his face; and they said, Behold, we *be* thy servants. And Joseph said unto them, Fear not: for *am* I in the place of God? But as for you, ye thought evil against me; *but* God meant it unto good, to bring to pass, as *it is* this day, to save much people alive. Now therefore fear ye not: I will nourish you, and your little ones. And he comforted them, and spake kindly unto them.

Genesis 50:15-21

Your destiny in God is not to become some mean, old, bitter, and vindictive person, that goes about destroying other people's dreams, visions, and lives. Forgiveness cannot be contingent on your feelings or emotions. Forgiveness is a decision; it is an act of faith. In Luke chapter seventeen, Jesus taught on offense and forgiveness. He told the disciples that if someone offended them, but repented and ask them for forgiveness, they were to forgive them, even if it happened seven times a day. The response of the disciples is noteworthy. They said, "Lord, Increase our faith."

Then said he unto the disciples, It is impossible but that offences will come: but

woe *unto him*, through whom they come! It were better for him that a millstone were hanged about his neck, and he cast into the sea, than that he should offend one of these little ones. Take heed to yourselves: If thy brother trespass against thee, rebuke him; and if he repent, forgive him. And if he trespass against thee seven times in a day, and seven times in a day turn again to thee, saying, I repent; thou shalt forgive him. And the apostles said unto the Lord, Increase our faith.

Luke 17:1-5

The Bible tells us not to be bitter and full of malice towards one another. It tells us to be kind hearted, and forgiving towards one another, just as God for Christ's sake has forgiven us. It takes faith to bring our dreams and visions to pass. However, an unforgiving attitude will hinder your faith, and therefore your dreams and visions. The Bible also tells us that when we pray, we must forgive others if we expect our prayers to be answered. We certainly will not see our dreams and visions come to pass without an effective prayer life. The Word of God also tells husbands not to be bitter against their wives, and to treat them with honor, so the husband's prayer will not be hindered. Consider the following scriptures that support this.

Let all bitterness, and wrath, and anger, and clamour, and evil speaking, be put away from you, with all malice: And be ye kind one to another, tenderhearted, forgiving one another, even as God for Christ's sake hath forgiven you.

Ephesians 4:31

Husbands, love *your* wives, and be not bitter against them.

Colossians 3:19

For verily I say unto you, That whosoever shall say unto this mountain, Be thou removed, and be thou cast into the sea; and shall not doubt in his heart, but shall believe that those things which he saith shall come to pass; he shall have whatsoever he saith. Therefore I say unto you, What things soever ye desire, when ye pray, believe that ye receive *them*, and ye shall have *them*. And when ye stand praying, forgive, if ye have ought against any: that your Father also which is in heaven may forgive you your trespasses. But if ye do not forgive, neither will your Father which is in heaven forgive your trespasses.

Mark 11:23--26

Likewise, ye husbands, dwell with *them* according to knowledge, giving honour unto the wife, as unto the weaker vessel, and as being heirs together of the grace of life; that your prayers be not hindered.

1 Peter 3:7

When Righteousness Answers

Joseph was a man of integrity and he walked uprightly before God. Through all the hurts and betrayals, Joseph believed God would answer in righteousness the injustices done to him. He believed righteousness would answer! Sometimes people don't want to forgive others because they feel like the unrighteousness done to them will never be answered. The world is full of injustice, hurts, wrongs, misuse and abuse. Rest assured however, righteousness will answer every situation and circumstance. Sometimes we think, or feel, as though things will never be made right when people do us wrong. However, I want you to know, righteousness will answer. If not in time, then in eternity. Righteousness is built into God's system. God will judge the world in righteousness.

For as the earth bringeth forth her bud, and as the garden causeth the things that are sown in it to spring forth; so the Lord GOD will cause

righteousness and praise to spring forth before all the nations.

Isaiah 61:11

Let the floods clap *their* hands: let the hills be joyful together" Before the LORD; for he cometh to judge the earth: with righteousness shall he judge the world, and the people with equity.

Psalm 98:8-9

Righteousness is conformity of heart and life to the divine will and law of God. It is uprightness before God. Sometimes people think they are getting away with some things, but righteousness will answer. Walk uprightly before the Lord. Do the right thing. Joseph walked uprightly before the Lord. He did what was right, even when he was done wrong! I believe it was Joseph's integrity, and uprightness before God, that protected him, and delivered him out of the pit and the prison.

The integrity of the upright shall guide them: but the perverseness of transgressors shall destroy them. Riches profit not in the day of wrath: but righteousness delivereth from death. The righteousness of the perfect shall direct his way: but the wicked shall fall by his own wickedness. The righteousness of the

upright shall deliver them: but transgressors shall be taken in *their own* naughtiness.

Proverbs 11:3-6

When David called on the Lord, he expected God to answer him in righteousness. He believed God is a faithful and righteous God, and will have mercy on us and answer our prayers in righteousness.

Hear me when I call, O God of my righteousness: thou hast enlarged me *when I was* in distress; have mercy upon me, and hear my prayer.

Psalm 4:1

Hear my prayer, O LORD, give ear to my supplications: IN THY FAITHFULNESS ANSWER ME, *and* IN THY RIGHTEOUSNESS [my emphasis].

Psalm 143:1

Jacob was another person who understood this principle of righteousness. Jacob fled his home because he had taken his brother Esau's birth right, and Esau had plans to kill him. Jacob fled to his uncle Laban's house and fell in love with his daughter Rachel. Jacob was no slouch when it came to deception, but he found out his uncle Laban was the "Mack Daddy" of deception! Jacob had an encounter with

Chapter 5

God on his way to Laban's house as he slept one night. He dreamed and saw a ladder set up on earth that reached to heaven, and he saw angels ascending and descending on it. He saw and heard the Lord speak to him, confirming the covenant with him, that He made with Abraham and his father Isaac. When Jacob woke, he said this place is none other but the house of God, and called the place Bethel. Jacob vowed to trust, serve, and be a faithful tither to God.

Jacob had shifted from his deceptive ways. Unfortunately, now he was faced with his uncle Laban, who had no such encounter! As I mentioned earlier, Jacob fell in love with Rachel and served Laban seven years so he could marry her. At the end of seven years, Laban threw Jacob a party, most likely got him drunk, slipped in Rachel's older sister into the bedroom, and Jacob woke up with a wife that was not part of the agreement. Laban explained to Jacob that in that culture, he could not give the younger daughter before the older one. Once again, Jacob entered into another agreement with Laban to serve him another seven years for Rachel, whom he loved. After Rachel gave birth to Joseph, Jacob asked Laban to release him, his wives, and children, because he had fulfilled their agreement. However, Laban saw how the Lord had blessed his household because of Jacob, so he offered to pay Jacob whatever wages he desired if he would stay.

Jacob reminded Laban how small his herds were before he served him, and how the Lord blessed Laban, and increased his herd since Jacob had come to serve him. Jacob struck a deal with Laban stating he would continue to serve Laban and keep his herds. However, his wages would be all the speckled and spotted cattle, brown sheep, and the spotted and speckled goats that were born [they would belong to Jacob]. Jacob didn't want any wages directly from Laban. He knew God would bless him. Jacob knew his uncle was the "Mack Daddy" of deception, and could not be trusted, so he said, "So shall my righteousness answer for me in the time to come..." and Laban agreed.

Give *me* my wives and my children, for whom I have served thee, and let me go: for thou knowest my service which I have done thee And Laban said unto him, I pray thee, if I have found favour in thine eyes, *tarry: for* I have learned by experience that the LORD hath blessed me for thy sake. And he said, Appoint me thy wages, and I will give *it*. And he said unto him, Thou knowest how I have served thee, and how thy cattle was with me. For *it was* little which thou hadst before I *came*, and it is *now* increased unto a multitude; and the LORD hath blessed thee since my coming: and now when shall I provide for mine own house also? And he said, What shall I give thee? And

Jacob said, Thou shalt not give me any thing: if thou wilt do this thing for me, I will again feed *and* keep thy flock. I will pass through all thy flock to day, removing from thence all the speckled and spotted cattle, and all the brown cattle among the sheep, and the spotted and speckled among the goats: and *of such* shall be my hire. So shall my righteousness answer for me in time to come, when it shall come for my hire before thy face: every one that *is* not speckled and spotted among the goats, and brown among the sheep, that shall be counted stolen with me. And Laban said, Behold, I would it might be according to thy word.

Genesis 30:26-34

After they made the agreement, Laban had all the speckled and spotted goats, and sheep separated from his herds, and gave them to his sons. He removed them a three days journey from Jacob and himself, and Jacob fed and kept the rest of Laban's flocks. God blessed Jacob, and he increased exceedingly in cattle, maidservants, menservants, camels, and donkeys. Laban and his sons began to be hostile towards Jacob because of all the prosperity God had blessed him with, through the birth of the spotted and speckled cattle, goats and sheep. Laban had changed Jacobs wages ten times [he kept changing the agreement, but God would cause the cattle, goats, and sheep, to be born according to each new agreement in Jacobs favor]. Jacob had a dream of God prospering him. God told Jacob He saw what Laban had done to him. God answered in righteousness! It is not a matter of "if" God will answer in righteousness, but "when" God answers in righteousness. God will prosper us in our dreams and visions, even though we have to deal with the Labans of the world. Just trust God, walk in forgiveness, and know that your righteousness will answer for you in time to come!

And your father hath deceived me, and changed my wages ten times; but God suffered him not to hurt me If he said thus, The speckled shall be thy wages; then all the cattle bare speckled: and if he said thus, The ringstreaked shall be thy hire; then bare all the cattle ringstreaked.

Thus God hath taken away the cattle of your father, and given *them* to me And it came to pass at the time that the cattle conceived, that I lifted up mine eyes, and saw in a dream, and, behold, the rams which leaped upon the cattle *were* ringstreaked, speckled, and grisled. And the angel of God spake unto me in a dream, *saying*, Jacob: And I said, Here *am* I.

And he said, Lift up now thine eyes, and see, all the rams which leap upon the cattle *are* ringstreaked, speckled, and grisled: for I have seen all that Laban doeth unto thee.

Genesis 31:7-12

Chapter 6

A PROBLEM SOLVING ATTITUDE

**People with a
"sent" attitude see
problems as opportunities
to excel.**

Like Joseph, everyone has a problem or faces a problem in life. Though Joseph had a God-given dream in his heart, he had family problems, pit problems (put in a pit by his brothers with the intent to kill him), freedom problems (he was sold into slavery twice), legal problems (falsely accused of sexual assault), and prison problems (thrown in prison because of false accusation). The presence of a genuine dream or vision from God does not mean the absence of problems. Joseph obviously had a problem solving attitude because he kept rising above them. Most people hate problems, and when initially faced with one, immediately find themselves in the dumps. They have a "here-we-go-again" attitude. People with a "sent" attitude see problems as opportunities to excel.

I have discovered there is no getting around problems in life. I have found that:

1. Finding a solution to my problems;
2. The length of time it takes me to solve my problems;
3. Receiving the resources I need to solve my problems;
4. And the degree of joy and peace I have in the midst (process of solving) of my problems;
   is greatly influenced by attitude!

A problem can be defined as any question or matter involving doubt, uncertainty, or difficulty. Generally speaking, we would say a problem is a bad situation. We use a number of words to describe our problems: complications; can of worms; dilemma; disagreement; hot water; headache; issue; mess; obstacle; pickle; and trouble. If I left your favorite one out, please forgive me. From a Christian perspective, problems are trials and tribulations, which are hardships that test our faith.

These things I have spoken unto you, that in me ye might have peace. In the world ye shall have tribulation: but be of good cheer; I have overcome the world.

John 16:33

And when they had preached the gospel to that city, and had taught many, they returned again to Lystra, and *to* Iconium, and Antioch, Confirming the souls of the disciples, *and* exhorting them to continue in the faith, and that we must through much tribulation enter into the kingdom of God.

Acts 14:22

Your attitude greatly impacts your problem solving ability. We must learn to choose what attitude we will have when confronted with a problem. Attitudes can be difficult to grasp because they are not really tangible objects. They are complex mental and psychological characteristics of a person's way of thinking, interpreting, evaluating, and learning to deal with life's myriad problems. When initially confronted with problems, we must not allow the following various emotions to overtake us: fear, anger, sadness, disappointment, shame, failure, bitterness or guilt. Persistent, prolonged, and suppressed (buried, but alive) negative emotions, often lead to a negative attitude towards life.

SENT OR SOLD: THE DREAMER'S DILEMMA

Sometimes, when we are confronted with a problem, we find ourselves with an attitude of selfishness (instead of being other-focused).Or, we find ourselves with a pessimistic attitude, instead of an optimistic one. It's important to remember that people pay us for the problems we solve in life. I have a Bachelor's Degree in Electrical Engineering. An engineer, in generic terms, is simply a problem solver! Corporations paid me for the problems I help them solve, not because I held the title of engineer. I had to develop a problem solving attitude, not just problem solving skills to be successful. People who solve, or help solve other people's problems, receive the greatest rewards (favor).

Selfish people are not very good problem solvers. They are only interested in solutions that benefit themselves. Selfish people always want help (want their problems to be solved), but rarely want to help (put forth effort) solve other people's problems. People who solve, or help solve other people's problems, receive help with their own problems. People with a "sold" attitude are pessimistic. They have a "not again," "can't get ahead for all my problems," attitude. People with a "sent" attitude are optimistic. They have a "something good is...," "there is a solution...," "I will solve this problem," attitude. When there seems to be no apparent way out of their problem, or dilemma, people with a "sent" attitude believe God will intervene, and provide a solution to their problems.

Chapter 6

There hath no temptation taken you but such as is common to man: but God *is* faithful, who will not suffer you to be tempted above that ye are able; but will with the temptation also make a way to escape, that ye may be able to bear *it*.

1 Corinthians 10:13

Joseph definitely had a problem solving attitude. Joseph obviously had problems of his own, but while in prison he noticed the down-hearted look on the face of Pharaoh's chief butler and chief baker. They had both dreamed a dream, and could not interpret it. Joseph then used his gifts, talents, and skills to interpret their dreams. Things turned out to be just as Joseph had said. Things did not work out so well for the chief baker, but that's another story. Anyway, what I want you to take away from this story is the unselfish problem solving attitude of Joseph. Again, Joseph had his own problems. He was sold into slavery by his own brothers; in a strange country, and thrown in prison because of false accusations. Why should he care about someone else's problems? Even in the midst of his own hardships, troubles, and tribulations, Joseph was willing to use his gifts and talents to serve, or help others.

People with a problem solving attitude may find themselves facing a setback, but their "sent" attitude will always pave the way for a comeback! A problem solving attitude will often lead to promotion. Joseph was a slave in

Potiphar's house, but he was promoted to overseer of Potiphar's entire household. Although Joseph was thrown into prison, the keeper of the prison promoted Joseph to Director of the prison. Ultimately, Joseph's unselfish problem solving attitude led to his release from prison, and his promotion to second in command over all of Egypt. Pharaoh too, had dreamed a dream that required interpretation. The chief butler whom Joseph had two years earlier properly interpreted his dream, remembered Joseph, and told Pharaoh about him. Pharaoh called for Joseph out of the prison, Joseph interpreted his dream in-which Pharaoh saw the wisdom of God in him, and promoted Joseph to second in command. A problem solving attitude will bring promotion and prosperity to you.

> **A problem solving attitude will bring promotion and prosperity to you.**

David's Problem Solving Attitude

Like Joseph, we can see some key problem solving attitudes in David's life. David experienced many problems in his life. He caused a few for himself. Haven't we all! Just the same, David was a problem solver. Problems challenge us all, especially big ones and life threatening ones. David faced a big problem called Goliath. Let's read about it from the Scriptures:

And there went out a champion out of the camp of the Philistines, named Goliath, of Gath, whose height *was* six cubits and a span. And *he had* an helmet of brass upon his head, and he *was* armed with a coat of mail; and the weight of the coat *was* five thousand shekels of brass. And *he had* greaves of brass upon his legs, and a target of brass between his shoulders. And the staff of his spear *was* like a weaver's beam; and his spear's head *weighed* six hundred shekels of iron: and one bearing a shield went before him. And he stood and cried unto the armies of Israel, and said unto them, Why are ye come out to set *your* battle in array? *am* not I a Philistine, and ye servants to Saul? choose you a man for you, and let him come down to me. If he be able to fight with me, and to kill me, then will we be your servants: but if I prevail against him, and kill him, then shall ye be our servants, and serve us. And the Philistine said, I defy the armies of Israel this day; give me a man, that we may fight together. When Saul and all Israel heard

those words of the Philistine, they were dismayed, and greatly afraid.

1 Samuel 17:1-11

King Saul and Israel's army was set for battle with the Philistines. Then Goliath, a giant, came forth with a challenge to King Saul and all of Israel. Goliath challenged them to send a man out to fight with him, and whoever won the fight would rule over the other nation. This challenge from Goliath brought great fear to Saul and his entire army. A challenge is a call to engage in a contest, fight, or competition. It is a call to confrontation. A Challenge calls for use of one's ability, or resources in a difficult, but stimulating effort. We feel challenged according to the degree or estimation of our deficiencies, or lack of ability and resources. Initial confrontation with problems often produce negative emotions (fear, etc.), that can lead to a negative attitude towards life if not dealt with.

Now David *was* the son of that Ephrathite of Bethlehemjudah, whose name *was* Jesse; and he had eight sons: and the man went among men *for* an old man in the days of Saul. And the three eldest sons of Jesse went *and* followed Saul to the battle: and the names of his three sons that went to the battle *were* Eliab the firstborn, and next unto him Abinadab, and the third Shammah. And

Chapter 6

**David *was* the youngest: and the three eldest
followed Saul. But David went and returned
from Saul to feed his father's sheep at
Bethlehem. And the Philistine drew near
morning and evening, and presented himself
forty days.**

1 Samuel 17:12-16

Goliath challenged Saul and his army for forty days.
Problems usually don't just go away because we ignore
them. The length of time it takes to solve our problems is
greatly influenced by our attitude. David's father asked him to
go check on his brothers who were in the army and to take
them some food. When David got to the camp, Goliath was
still spewing out his challenge. Problems have a voice (they
talk to you), and they say the same words to you until they
are dealt with or solved.

**And David left his carriage in the hand of the
keeper of the carriage, and ran into the army,
and came and saluted his brethren. And as he
talked with them, behold, there came up the
champion, the Philistine of Gath, Goliath by
name, out of the armies of the Philistines, and
spake according to the same words: and David
heard *them*. And all the men of Israel, when
they saw the man, fled from him, and were
sore afraid.**

1 Samuel 17:22-24

David also learned that a problem solving attitude will bring promotion and prosperity into your life. King Saul had offered his daughter in marriage to the man who would go and fight with Goliath and kill him. In addition, he would receive great riches and be free from taxes for the rest of his life. Generally speaking, the bigger the problem, the bigger the reward! People with a problem solving attitude will see a bigger reward over a bigger problem. David's problem solving attitude was an outgrowth of his relationship with God. He saw himself as being in covenant with God. David had respect and honor for covenant relationship with God. Whenever he faced a problem, especially a big one like Goliath, David expected God to help him solve it. Saul, and the men of Israel's army saw their problem (Goliath) in light of their own abilities, but David saw their problem in light of God's ability! David's attitude was this problem is not just about defying Israel, it's about defying Israel and the Living God.

> **And the men of Israel said, Have ye seen this man that is come up? surely to defy Israel is he come up: and it shall be, *that* the man who killeth him, the king will enrich him with great riches, and will give him his daughter, and make his father's house free in Israel.**

> **And David spake to the men that stood by him, saying, What shall be done to the man**

that killeth this Philistine, and taketh away the reproach from Israel? For who *is* this uncircumcised Philistine, that he should defy the armies of the living God?

And the people answered him after this manner, saying, So shall it be done to the man that killeth him.

1 Samuel 17:25-27

People with a positive, problem solving attitude sometimes irritate those who don't have it, but should have it, when facing a problem. David's older brother Eliab became angry (negative emotion) at David because he (Eliab) was fearful (negative emotion), and David was talking courageously. The attitude of courage does not come automatically with age or training. Saul and his army were trained men in fighting. Perhaps Eliab felt shame (negative emotion), because his little brother showed more courage than himself. People with a courageous attitude towards life, are often viewed as prideful by those who are fearful. Eliab's attitude towards David was not based on this one incident, but on David's reputation. Before David's confrontation with Eliab, Saul had requested a skillful musician to come and play for him. Even then, David had a reputation of being courageous and his older brother knew David's true character.

And Saul said unto his servants, Provide me now a man that can play well, and bring *him* to me. Then answered one of the servants, and said, Behold, I have seen a son of Jesse the Bethlehemite, *that is* cunning in playing, and a mighty valiant man, and a man of war, and prudent in matters, and a comely person, and the LORD *is* with him.

1 Samuel 16:17-18

And Eliab his eldest brother heard when he spake unto the men; and Eliab's anger was kindled against David, and he said, Why camest thou down hither? and with whom hast thou left those few sheep in the wilderness? I know thy pride, and the naughtiness of thine heart; for thou art come down that thou mightest see the battle. And David said, What have I now done? *Is there* not a cause? And he turned from him toward another, and spake after the same manner: and the people answered him again after the former manner.

1 Samuel 17:28-30

Chapter 6

The attitude of courage is a problem solving attitude.

A problem solving attitude will not be discouraged by the negative attitude of others. Problem solvers put very little weight on the words of discouragers, even when they are family. As we just read above, after Eliab spoke in a discouraging manner to David, David simply turned from him and continued his conversation with another. The attitude of courage is a problem solving attitude. An attitude of courage and optimism in the face of problems will open up opportunities for you. When King Saul heard about David's problem solving attitude, he sent for David.

> **And when the words were heard which David spake, they rehearsed *them* before Saul: and he sent for him.**
>
> **1 Samuel 17:31**

When David came before King Saul, he spoke confidently about his ability to deal with the big problem at hand. Saul told David he was just a youth and no match for Goliath who was a man of war from his youth. Saul's words to David were based solely on the flesh and not faith and spirit. People with a problem solving attitude must constantly overcome discouragement and confidence based solely on the flesh. David's attitude was he had faced and defeated problems bigger than himself before, with the help of the Lord, and things would be no different with this un-covenanted Philistine. David had already killed a lion and a bear with God's help. David's attitude was, my problems may change or get bigger, but my principles, attitude, and my God remain the same!

> **And David said unto Saul, Thy servant kept his father's sheep, and there came a lion, and a bear, and took a lamb out of the flock: And I went out after him, and smote him, and delivered *it* out of his mouth: and when he arose against me, I caught *him* by his beard, and smote him, and slew him. Thy servant slew both the lion and the bear: and this uncircumcised Philistine shall be as one of them, seeing he hath defied the armies of the living God. David said moreover, The LORD that delivered me out of the paw of the lion, and out of the paw of the bear, he will deliver me out of the hand of this Philistine.**
>
> **1 Samuel 17:34-37**

David's attitude invoked a God-consciousness in King Saul. He told David to "Go, and the Lord be with you!" People with a problem solving attitude use proven, but often un-conventional means to solve their problems. King Saul tried to get David to use his traditional sword and armor to fight Goliath, but David refused them, and chose to use what he did when he killed the lion and the bear. Instead, he girded up himself with his staff, five smooth stones, his shepherd's bag, and his sling.

And Saul armed David with his armour, and he put an helmet of brass upon his head; also he armed him with a coat of mail. And David girded his sword upon his armour, and he assayed to go; for he had not proved *it*. And David said unto Saul, I cannot go with these; for I have not proved *them*. And David put them off him. And he took his staff in his hand, and chose him five smooth stones out of the brook, and put them in a shepherd's bag which he had, even in a scrip; and his sling *was* in his hand: and he drew near to the Philistine. And the Philistine came on and drew near unto David; and the man that bare the shield *went* before him.

1 Samuel 17:38-41

Problem solvers face constant discouragement from the problem itself. David was armed and ready for battle, but Goliath belittled him and threatened him. Again, problems have a voice, and will speak discouragement to you. Big problems, like Goliath, have big mouths! However, don't let them intimidate you. David in return, spoke back to his problem. He spoke the solution and not the problem. He invoked the name of the Lord. He had a confident attitude that God would help him with this giant size problem. Like David, people with a problem solving attitude don't run from their problems, they run towards them, to remove or solve them. David ran towards Goliath, hit him in the forehead with a stone from his sling, and knocked him to the ground. He then ran to Goliath lying on the ground, took Goliath's own sword and cut off his head. Problem solved!

And when the Philistine looked about, and saw David, he disdained him: for he was *but* a youth, and ruddy, and of a fair countenance. And the Philistine said unto David, *Am* I a dog, that thou comest to me with staves? And the Philistine cursed David by his gods. And the Philistine said to David, Come to me, and I will give thy flesh unto the fowls of the air, and to the beasts of the field. Then said David to the Philistine, Thou comest to me with a sword, and with a spear, and with a shield: but I come to thee in the name of the

LORD of hosts, the God of the armies of Israel, whom thou hast defied. This day will the LORD deliver thee into mine hand; and I will smite thee, and take thine head from thee; and I will give the carcases of the host of the Philistines this day unto the fowls of the air, and to the wild beasts of the earth; that all the earth may know that there is a God in Israel. And all this assembly shall know that the LORD saveth not with sword and spear: for the battle *is* the LORD'S, and he will give you into our hands. And it came to pass, when the Philistine arose, and came and drew nigh to meet David, that David hasted, and ran toward the army to meet the Philistine. And David put his hand in his bag, and took thence a stone, and slang *it*, and smote the Philistine in his forehead, that the stone sunk into his forehead; and he fell upon his face to the earth. So David prevailed over the Philistine with a sling and with a stone, and smote the Philistine, and slew him; but *there was* no sword in the hand of David. Therefore David ran, and stood upon the Philistine, and took his sword, and drew it out of the sheath thereof, and slew him, and cut off his head therewith. And when the Philistines saw their champion was dead, they fled.

1 Samuel 17:42-52

Chapter 7

THE ELLIPSIS FACTOR

To fulfill our God-given dreams and visions we often have to deal with what I call "The Ellipsis Factor," or "The Dot-Dot-Dot Factor." This is when God gives you the beginning and end of your assignment, dream, or vision, but omits the middle portion of the experience! Joseph knew his beginning (where he was at), and he knew his end would be an exalted position from his dreams. However, God didn't mention anything about the pit, being sold twice, or being put into prison! In grammatical terms, an ellipsis is the omission of a word, or words for the syntactical construction of a sentence, but not necessary for understanding it. It is a mark or series of marks "..." used in writing or printing to indicate an omission of a word or words; hence, the "Dot-Dot-Dot." factor!

Let me now give you my definition of the ellipsis factor from a faith and spiritual perspective. It is the element of omission of some details concerning our lives, dreams, visions, and assignments from God; necessary for the completion of fulfillment, but not necessary for understanding the assignment. Again, God had revealed to Joseph in his dream that his destiny would be one of leadership and authority, even over his parents and brothers. Joseph understood what his dream meant, even though he did not have all the details of the pit and prison experience. Like the disciples in Mark, chapter four and six, God will tell you to go to the other side, but not mention a storm will arise before you get to the other side!

And the same day, when the even was come, he saith unto them, Let us pass over unto the other side. And when they had sent away the multitude, they took him even as he was in the ship. And there were also with him other little ships. And there arose a great storm of wind, and the waves beat into the ship, so that it was now full.

And he was in the hinder part of the ship, asleep on a pillow: and they awake him, and say unto him, Master, carest thou not that we perish? And he arose, and re-buked the wind, and said unto the sea, Peace, be still. And the

wind ceased, and there was a great calm. And he said unto them, Why are ye so fearful? how is it that ye have no faith? And they feared exceedingly, and said one to another, What manner of man is this, that even the wind and the sea obey him?

Mark 4:35-41

And straightway he constrained his disciples to get into the ship, and to go to the other side before unto Bethsaida, while he sent away the people. And when he had sent them away, he departed into a mountain to pray.

And when even was come, the ship was in the midst of the sea, and he alone on the land. And he saw them toiling in rowing; for the wind was contrary unto them: and about the four cometh unto them, walking upon the sea, and would have passed by them. But when they saw him walking upon the sea, they supposed it had been a spirit, and cried out: For they all saw him, and were troubled.

And immediately he talked with them, and saith unto them, Be of good cheer: it is I; be not afraid. And he went up unto them into the ship; and the wind ceased: and they were sore

amazed in themselves beyond measure, and wondered. For they considered not the miracle of the loaves: for their heart was hardened.

Mark 6:45-52

Like Joseph, God may give you a dream that releases a sense of destiny in your life, but omit some details, such as the pit or the prison. It is especially during these times we must maintain a "sent" attitude. God gives us the headlines, and even the outlines, but the details unfold before us as we walk by faith! We still have to negotiate and navigate the details of our dreams, visions, and assignments from God to complete or fulfill them, even though it is not necessary for us to know the details before time, in order to understand our assignments. It is during those times of negotiating and navigating the unknown details of our assignments from God, that we sometimes began to lose our focus, and confidence, and therefore abort our assignments and destiny in God.

We must learn to deal with the "dot-dot-dot" factor! In other words we must learn to deal with the omitted details; the unknown details; the things we didn't see coming. To deal with the "dot-dot-dot" factor requires us to do three basic things: (1)Remind yourself of God's reference point, (2)Get a fresh/new revelation of God's character and purpose in our life, and (3) See yourself as sent and not sold!

Chapter 7

Remind Yourself of God's Reference Point

When God gives you a dream, vision, or assignment, it will challenge your faith. If you go by your present circumstances, or details, it may cause you to abort your God-given destiny. God knows the end from the very beginning, and will deal with you accordingly. It can be very frustrating when you are obviously struggling, and God speaks to your heart, through His Word, and by His Spirit, as though you have already won! Sometimes we can begin to think it is God who doesn't get it, or He really doesn't care about our present condition. The truth is, God's reference point for what we are facing, is often different from our own. To exercise faith, and cooperate with God, we must learn to operate from God's reference point. Remember when God sent an angel to Gideon, and called him a mighty man of valor. Gideon was hiding in the winepress like a coward. I image Gideon was thinking, "You talking to me?" Perhaps he was thinking, "Uh, excuse me Sir, you must have the wrong fellow!" God's reference point is not who you are now, but who He has called you to be!

**God's reference point
is not who you are now,
but who He has called
you to be!**

> **And there came an angel of the LORD, and sat under an oak which *was* in Ophrah, that *pertained* unto Joash the Abiezrite: and his son Gideon threshed wheat by the winepress, to hide *it* from the" Midianites. And the angel of the LORD appeared unto him, and said unto him, The LORD *is* with thee, thou mighty man of valour.**
>
> **Judges 6:11-12**

God knows the end of the matter from the beginning. He already sees you as victorious. He already sees beyond your present challenges and problems. He is a God that calls those things that be not as though they are. God's reference point is not your present condition, but your promised inheritance. God's reference point is not where you are at right now, but where he has sent you!

> **And the LORD looked upon him, and said, Go in this thy might, and thou shalt save Israel from the hand of the Midianites: have not I sent thee?**
>
> **Judges 6:14**

Chapter 7

Get a Fresh Revelation of God's Character

God had given Moses his assignment to deliver His people out of Egypt, and from under Pharaoh's thumb. Moses was at a point in his assignment where not only had Pharaoh rejected his leadership, but Israel (his own people) also rejected him. Moses began to question God's plan for his life. God began to strengthen Moses heart by giving him a fresh, or new revelation, of who He is! God told Moses that He was previously only known by the name of "God Almighty" or El-Shaddai. However, God was now revealing Himself to Moses in a way not previously known. He was now revealing Himself as JEHOVAH! He was now revealing Himself to Moses as a promise-keeper or covenant keeper. Moses needed to get a revelation that He is the God who never changes and whose promise never fail. Sometimes when we get stuck in our faith, what we really need is a fresh revelation of God's character. Instead of begging God to deliver us, sometimes we just need to do a character study on God from the word of God (The Bible).

> **Sometimes when we get stuck in our faith, what we really need is a fresh revelation of God's character.**

> **And God spake unto Moses, and said unto him, I *am* the LORD: And I appeared unto Abraham, unto Isaac, and unto Jacob, by *the name of* God Almighty, but by my name Jehovah was I not known to them.**
>
> **Exodus 6:2-3**

> **And Moses and Aaron did as the LORD commanded them, so did they.**
>
> **Exodus 7:6**

When you get a fresh revelation of who God is, it will empower you to complete your assignment from God. Make getting to know God a priority in your life, and especially during times of trials and tribulations. In the midst of your trials and tribulations, as you pursue your dreams and visions, expect God to reveal Himself to you in new ways.

See Yourself as Sent and Not Sold

As you negotiate and navigate the "dot-dot-dot" factor, allow your dreams and visions to inspire you to a "sent" attitude. Don't allow the surprise and difficulties of those unknown details push you into a "sold" mentality. People with a "sold" mentality see themselves as being in bondage to their circumstances. Leaders who develop a "sold" mindset will consistently abort their assignments from God. However, Joseph did not abort his dreams and visions. He did not surrender his destiny to a "sold" attitude. Joseph was sold into slavery, not once, but twice. Yet, he saw himself as being sent by God.

Now therefore be not grieved, nor angry with yourselves, that ye sold me hither: for God did send me before you to preserve life.

Genesis 45:5

> **Yes, in the natural, his circumstances said he was "sold," but his attitude said he was "sent" by God!**

Yes, in the natural, his circumstances said he was "sold," but his attitude said he was "sent" by God! Joseph's "sent" attitude allowed him to walk in forgiveness with his brothers, even though they had mistreated him, and sold him into slavery. People with a "sent" attitude, walk in forgiveness. Are you struggling with the ellipsis (dot-dot-dot) factor in your life? Are you wrestling with the "Dreamer's Dilemma" in your life? Maybe it's time for a new attitude!

Chapter 8

A NEW ATTITUDE

In Saint John, chapter 17, the Lord Jesus Christ prayed for his disciples. In verse 18 of John, chapter 17, Jesus makes it clear that as the Father has sent Him, even so has He sent us into the world as His disciples.

As thou hast sent me into the world, even so have I also sent them into the world.

John 17:18

Jesus is saying that His disciples (the Church), are sent into the world with the same mission, purpose, and results as himself. Just as Joseph was sent to Egypt to be a deliverer, even so, God has sent us into the world in Christ, to bring salvation to the world. Remember, you are sent by God! You are the light of the world and the salt of the earth. God has poured out His Spirit, and we have dreams and visions that propel us into our destinies like Joseph.

And it shall come to pass afterward, that I will pour out my spirit upon all flesh; and your sons and your daughters shall prophesy, your old men shall dream dreams, your young men shall see visions: And also upon the servants and upon the handmaids in those days will I pour out my spirit.

Joel 2:28-29

Like Joseph, we also face opposition, obstacles, trials, tribulations, and persecution. Even though Joseph had a God-given dream, he had to deal with envy and hatred, from his own family. He was put in a pit, sold twice into slavery, and falsely accused of sexual assault, which landed him in prison. Yet, Joseph's attitude was that he was sent by God, and not sold under his circumstances.

Oh, the power of a "sent" attitude! Joseph did not become bitter, or quit on his dreams. He walked uprightly before God, and did what was right, even though others were doing him wrong. Joseph walked in integrity. Joseph walked in forgiveness towards those who had done him wrong. In the end, Joseph was promoted and his dream fulfilled. Walking in forgiveness paves the way for us to keep moving forward in our dreams and visions, regardless as to how others may treat us. I believe God wants you and me to have the same "sent" attitude as Joseph; regardless of the difficulties of our circumstances.

> **I believe God wants you and me to have the same "sent" attitude as Joseph; regardless of the difficulties of our circumstances.**

As believers, we should have the mind of Christ. In other words, we must learn to think like Jesus. The Bible tells us to be renewed in the attitude of our minds.

And be renewed in the spirit of your mind;
Ephesians 4:23

to be made new in the attitude of your minds;
Ephesians 4:23 (NIV)

And be constantly renewed in the spirit of your mind [having a fresh mental and spiritual attitude],
Ephesians 4:23 (AMP)

SENT OR SOLD: THE DREAMER'S DILEMMA

Perhaps it is time for a new attitude in your life. Jesus said, we would have troubles in this world, but to be of good cheer, because He has overcome the world. Don't allow yourself to develop a "sold" mindset. It is time to resolve the "Dreamer's Dilemma" in your own life. It is time to agree and decree God's word: God is with me... He will deliver me... God gives me favor... and God will give me wisdom. In spite of your challenges, declare you are an overcomer and a winner! Decide here and now, once-and-for-all, that your attitude is "I am sent by God, and not sold under my circumstances!"

www.ingramcontent.com/pod-product-compliance
Lightning Source LLC
Chambersburg PA
CBHW060942040426

42445CB00011B/972